RECIPES FROM
THE HEART OF DIXIE

DAUGHTERS OF UTAH PIONEERS

Contributors

Joan Silver

Marlene Wood

Gail Smith

Maxine Humphrey

Lucile Larson

Ruth Snarr

Wendy Swanson

Judy Buckles

Gail Ann Jacobsen

Jan Slocum

Tamara Rogers

Norma Dooley

Pat Magleby

Anna Frezza

Judy Call

Margaret Vowles

Cover photo courtesy of: https://www.publicdomainpictures.net/en/view-image.php?image=76584&picture=vintage-kitchen-painting-scene

Published by Swanson Literary Group

ISBN: 9781795774604

DEDICATION

To all the mothers, sisters, grandmothers and friends that shared their love and love of cooking with us.

"The recipe that is not shared with others will soon be forgotten, but when it is shared, it will be enjoyed by future generations."
Author Unknown

RECIPE FOR A GOOD FAMILY   Judy Call

One intelligent Father

A handful of loving grandparents

One forgiving Mother

A smattering of "mixed nuts"
   (commonly called children)

Several dozen good eggs
   (not hardboiled) called friends

A smooth bunch of relatives

Mix with some fun and plenty of common sense. Add generous amounts of diligence, foresightedness and cooperation. Use an unlimited supply of tact. Lastly add equal amounts of push, pull and pep. Use a light but firm hand and stir with enthusiasm. Sweeten the Mother occasionally with honeyed words. Use a soft soap on members and rub it in. (There is nothing like lubrication to prevent friction.) Introduce new ideas and allow them to simmer. Season with a yearly vacation. Mix all together with one big family reunion. Cover with glory and honor. Serve with hospitality and music.

CONTENTS

Statue at the Historic Relief Society Hall, Washington, Utah

PREFACE

Picture this: You've set out with your husband and children in search of a new home. Everything that you can think of that you may possibly need, and will fit, is in your ox-drawn wagon. Your family is one of the lucky ones; your husband knew that oxen, although slower, would hold up much better than a team of mules. The wagon train is following the Platte River and you're almost halfway to Zion; you'll reach Chimney Rock by nightfall. It's the last day in July and you've been on the trail for six weeks. Tomorrow, your company will be stopping for a few days; the stock need rest and there's an ample supply of grass and water there; you've heard that might not be case once you start into Wyoming. Your husband plans on going hunting and the older children are going exploring and fishing. You, on the other hand, will be doing what you've been doing all along; cooking, washing and mending clothing, tending the babies, keeping the wagon organized and in good order; but at least you'll be able to catch up on your sewing without being jostled along in a moving wagon over the bumpy trail.

To celebrate this short break, you're going to make a wilderness stew with dumplings and hopefully a pie for dessert! Up to this point, you've made a few cobblers for dessert, but not a real pie. Your oldest daughter has promised to look for ripe berries and taken a pail with her to gather them. So far on this trip your cooking has been in a Dutch oven or over an open fire. Everyone has been picking up pieces of firewood when they can, and you supplement it with buffalo chips.

Late the next morning after having arrived at Chimney Rock the previous evening, you've done the washing, the stew is set to cooking, and you've mended everyone's stockings; it's now time to get to work on that pie. To ensure that it will have a nice flaky crust; early this morning, you had placed some lard in the creek to cool. You very carefully measure out your flour and salt as they are becoming a scarce commodity and you don't want to waste a single grain. Now that you've cut the lard into the flour and added water, you have a lovely dough ready. You look around and wonder what on earth you're going to use to roll it out on. You decide to use the wagon seat; you've found it comes in handy for a work table, and it will work perfectly to roll out your dough! Your daughter, bless her heart, arrives back in camp with a pail of fat, ripe blackberries! You can now get that pie put together, and you're thankful that you didn't have to churn butter, because you had remembered to hang your churn with fresh milk in it to the side of the wagon the day before, and it is now churned!

The wilderness stew and dumplings were tasty; and you've made them often enough by now, you can do it with your eyes closed. Oh, and the blackberry pie was so delicious; your family is going to be asking, no, begging for another one all the way to your new home! You worked hard all day, but tomorrow is the Sabbath, so you'll get some rest then.

You've placed your faith in God and your leaders. You think about what you have endured and the better life your children will have in Utah; no more will your family and friends be persecuted and driven from their homes. There will be plenty of land to raise crops and cattle. Soon homes, schools and churches will be built. This long trip will be worth the sacrifices you have made thus far. Life will be good, food will be plenty, and you feel blessed.

Whether your ancestors crossed the plains on the Mormon, Oregon or California trails, they faced the same obstacles and challenges. For that matter, all of our ancestors were pioneers of some sort, as are many of us today.

The following thoughts about Utah pioneers were written by Gordon B. Hinckley in 1984 (he would later become a president of the Church of Jesus Christ of Latter Day Saints), but they are a superb description of all pioneers. "It is good to look to the past to gain appreciation for the present and perspective for the future. It is good to look upon the virtues of those who have gone before, to gain strength for whatever lies ahead. It is good to reflect upon the work of those who labored so hard and gained so little in this world, but out of whose dreams and early plans, so well nurtured, has come a great harvest of which we are the beneficiaries. Their tremendous example can become a compelling motivation for us all, for each of us is a pioneer in his own life, often in his own family, and many of us pioneer daily..."

As a member of the International Society Daughters of Utah Pioneers and amateur genealogist, I think about the generations that came before me quite often; when I write their histories, share their stories, but most often when I use recipes that have been handed down from mother to daughter, time and time again.

Wendy Warren Swanson

A BRIEF HISTORY OF UTAH'S "DIXIE"

When it became obvious that there was going to be a civil war in the United States; Brigham Young became concerned that cotton cloth, already hard to obtain in Utah in the 1850's, was going to become a scarce commodity, he asked the missionaries that were already in Southern Utah proselytizing to the Native American about the feasibility of growing cotton in the area. They reported yes; the climate was suitable for growing cotton and they began growing cotton on a small scale.

In 1857, the Robert Covington and Samuel Adair companies were formed and called to settle Southern Utah and grow cotton. The Adair Company arrived in March with 10 families and the Covington Company arrived in April with 28 families. They consisted of people who had roots in the Southern United States and most had experience in growing cotton. Because these families hailed from the South, Southern Utah was nicknamed Utah's "Dixie."

In 1861, six months after the civil war in the United States began, Brigham Young, at the October General Conference for the Church of Jesus Christ of Latter Day Saints, read the names of over 300 families that were also to be sent to Southern Utah to establish what became known as the "Dixie Cotton Mission."

The cotton industry in Southern Utah did poorly due to the heat and soil conditions and produced a disappointing crop. By the time the Washington Cotton Factory was complete, the civil war had ended and it was no longer practical or economical to grow cotton in Southern Utah. The industry had a short revival from 1873 to 1876 and again from 1893 to 1896. Some of the families from the "Dixie Cotton Mission" stayed and the area has remained Utah's "Dixie"

Washington Cotton Factory ~ Established 1865
Now the home of Star Nursery ~ Washington, Utah

MULBERRY TREES AND SILKWORMS IN DIXIE

How Mulberry Camp ~ Daughters of Utah Pioneers got its name:

SILK PRODUCTION (SERICULTURE) COMES TO UTAH!

When Brigham Young spent his 20-month mission for the Church of Jesus Chris of Latter-day Saints in Manchester, England in 1840 and 1841, he became interested in the silk weaving industry and became versed on the silk weaving looms.

These ancient arts descended from the Huguenots who emigrated from Lyons, France due to religious persecution. Perhaps Brigham Young felt an affinity to these people as he was experiencing persecution back in America?

Legend has it that the Greek emperor Justinian had two monks steal silkworm eggs out of China in the 6th century along with seeds from the Mulberry tree. Up until that time the Chinese had successfully guarded their secrets of making silk for ages!

An emperor's wife had accidentally dropped a silkworm cocoon into her tea cup and saw that it unraveled into the most exquisite thread she had ever seen.

Mulberry Tree
Dr. Avishai Teicher Pikiwiki Israel [CC BY 2.5 (https://creativecommons.org/licenses/by/2.5)]

In the 1860's Brigham Young imported 100,000 Mulberry trees from France to Utah. He also obtained silkworm eggs and had a model cocoonery for two million worms. He taught people the process of harvesting silkworms. He kept silkworms in his winter home in St. George and his wife Zina Diantha Huntington Young handed out small

Mulberry leaves, about an inch in diameter, complete with tiny silk worms!

The work of silkworm care and processing fell to the Relief Society of the church (the oldest female organization in the world), so it didn't take up the time of those suited for harder labor. Silk production took place primarily at the Cotton Mill in Washington County Utah.

The worms were carried in pouches hung around the Relief Society ladies necks or in their pocket to keep them warm until they hatched. The silkworms were then fed fresh Mulberry leaves for 40 days until they formed a cocoon. The cocoon was then boiled to kill the moth and then the ladies unraveled the nearly invisible thread with their fingers and coiled it around a paddle.

An American flag made of Utah silk was flown at the 1893 World's Fair in Chicago, Illinois. Also on display at the fair were dresses, scarves, shawls and a banner featuring the sego lily; all made from Utah silk.

It took 30,000 worms to make 12 pounds of raw silk; 2,500 cocoons to make just one pound of silk!

Silk weaving took place at the Washington cotton factory, which became a part of Zion's Cooperative Mercantile Institution (ZCMI). It served over 150 Utah communities with retail goods.

Washington Cotton Factory ~ Established 1865

This was an arduous process, so it ended. There are still many Mulberry trees in Washington County, Utah and that is where Mulberry Camp took its name. Be sure to take a look at the silkworm recipes in the "Miscellaneous" section of this book.

Mulberry Camp of Daughters of Utah Pioneers took the name "Mulberry" in honor of these ladies that worked so hard at the process of raising silk worms and turning the silk into cloth. Mulberry Camp has been in existence for almost 50 years, and we are part of the Washington East Company. Our members come from many walks of life. We are musicians, teachers, authors, entrepreneurs, artists, business owners and homemakers. We belong to the Washington East Company of Daughters of Utah Pioneers.

What do we have in common with one another? Our history! We are descendants of Utah Pioneers; we are descended from settlers, and fur trappers and traders, and miners, and railroaders and explorers. Whether our ancestors stayed in the Utah Territory; or just traveled through on their way to the California gold fields, or to take up homesteading in the Oregon Territory, where government and railroad land was free or almost free; or even ventured into Utah lands to trap and trade, or stayed only long enough to help build the transcontinental railroad; the "Daughters" have one common goal, and that is to "preserve the past and strengthen the future." That is why one of our most important responsibilities is to research and record the history of our Utah pioneer ancestors.

The International Society Daughters of Utah Pioneers (ISDUP) is a heritage organization. It exists solely for historical, educational and public purposes, and is completely non-political and non-sectarian.

All female direct-line descendants (or legally adopted direct-line descendants) of the pioneers that passed through the Utah Territory between July 1847 and the completion of the transcontinental railroad on May 10, 1869 are considered "Daughters of Utah Pioneers," and are eligible for membership in the "International Society Daughters of Utah Pioneers."

During the period between 1847 and 1869, the Utah Territory consisted of what are now Utah, Nevada, and parts of Wyoming and Colorado. So, you may be eligible for membership and not even realize it.

Daughters of Utah Pioneers ~ McQuarrie Memorial Museum ~ St. George, Utah

INTRODUCTION

Some of the recipes in this book have been handed down for generations; even back to our pioneer ancestors, but many we got from watching our mothers and grandmothers prepare meals and those oh so delicious treats! Many of these have never been written down; just passed down, sometimes by trial and error, from generation to generation. Also included are some of our favorite modern recipes.

Through this book we would like to share our recipes, some of them a secret until now, with our fellow bakers and cooks, as well as friends and family.

We have included several recipes for dishes that are somewhat unique to Utah: Frog Eye Salad, Funeral Potatoes, Green Jello Salad, Ambrosia Salad and anything made in a Dutch oven or crock pot. Dixie Salad, a recipe that is unique to Southern Utah is also included.

Relief Society Hall, Washington, Utah ~ Constructed in 1875

BREAKFAST

BREAKFAST

DUTCH OVEN SCRAMBLE WITH BISCUITS   Wendy Swanson

2 eggs per person
1 medium onion
Salt and pepper to taste
1 can Pillsbury buttermilk biscuits
Optional ingredients: tomato, crumbled bacon, green chili, etc.

1 bell pepper
Cayenne pepper
1/2 c. grated cheddar cheese

Prepare your heat source using wood or charcoal coals.

Chop pepper, onion and any other ingredients you like in your eggs. In a bowl, beat the eggs then add the pepper, onion and any optional ingredients. Season to taste with cayenne pepper, salt and pepper.

Place Dutch oven and lid over hot coals. Coat the oven sides and bottom with vegetable oil. Coat the oven lid with vegetable oil. Open the can of biscuits and lightly coat each side with oil. When the oven is hot, place the biscuits on the oven lid and then pour the egg mixture into the oven and replace the lid.

Remove the lid to stir the eggs from time to time, replacing the lid after stirring. When the bottom of the biscuits are browned, turn them over to cook the other side.

Sprinkle the grated cheese over the egg mixture a minute or two before the eggs are done and replace the lid.

When the biscuits are browned on both sides, remove the oven from the heat and serve.

Secret to success:

Plan more than you can do, then do it.
Bite off more than you can chew, then chew it.
Hitch your wagon to a star; keep your seat and there you are.

BREAKFAST

BANANA SOUR CREAM FRENCH TOAST   Wendy Swanson

4 eggs
3/4 c. milk
3/4 c. sour cream
1 banana, cut into small pieces
1/2 tsp. allspice
1 tsp. vanilla
16 thick slices of French bread (about one loaf)

Mix first six ingredients until smooth; dip bread into egg mix and set on a cookie sheet for 15 minutes.

Coat a large frying pan with oil and fry the bread until golden brown.

Serve with maple syrup, fresh bananas and strawberries.

BREAKFAST

EGGNOG PANCAKES
(Christmas – New Year)

Judy Call

1 1/3 c. flour
1/4 c. sugar
1 tsp. baking soda
1 egg
1 Tbsp. vegetable oil

1/8 tsp. cloves
1/4 tsp. nutmeg
1/2 tsp. salt
1 1/2 c. commercial eggnog
Option: red or green food coloring for festive look

Combine first 6 ingredients in a bowl. Set aside. Combine eggnog, egg and oil. Stir into dry ingredients, stirring just until moistened.

Pour 1/4 cup batter for each pancake onto a hot, lightly-greased griddle. Cook until top is covered with bubbles. Turn and cook on the other side.

Serve with butter and powdered sugar if desired. Yield is 12 (4 inch) pancakes.

These pancakes may be frozen. To freeze, stack pancakes between sheets of waxed paper. Place in airtight container. Freeze up to 1 month.

BREAKFAST

JOHN WAYNE CASSEROLE   Wendy Swanson

This recipe comes from an old friend of mine, who got it from an old friend of hers.

1 lb. mild cheddar cheese (grated)   1 lb. jack cheese (grated)
1 lg. can chopped Ortega chilies   4 egg yolks, beaten
1 sm. can evaporate milk   1 tsp. salt
1/8 tsp. pepper   1 Tbsp. flour
4 egg whites, beaten until stiff

Blend beaten egg yolks, evaporated milk, salt, pepper and flour. Set aside.

Mix grated cheese and chopped chilies together well. Put into a buttered 9x13" casserole dish.

Fold stiffly beaten egg whites into blended yolk mixture. Spoon over cheese mixture. Bake in a 350° oven until silver knife comes out clean; about 35 minutes. Do not over bake.

BREAKFAST

MEXICAN OMELET
(Gluten free)

Pat Magleby

Oil a 9 x 12 baking dish.

Layer in pan: 8 oz. shredded cheddar cheese
8 oz. shredded Monterey Jack cheese
4 oz. chopped green chilies (drained)

Beat 12 eggs. Add 16 oz. sour cream, 1/4 c. milk and 1 tsp. salt.

Pour gently over cheeses.

Bake at 350° for 45 minutes to 1 hour.

Can be topped with sliced tomatoes and parmesan cheese (reheat for a few minutes).

Let sit 5 minutes before cutting.

BREAKFAST

PUMPKIN WAFFLES AND HAZELNUT BUTTER   Wendy Swanson

2 1/4 c. flour
2 tsp. cinnamon
1 tsp. ginger
1/4 c. packed brown sugar
4 eggs, separated
1/4 c. butter, melted

4 tsp. baking powder
1 tsp. allspice
1/2 tsp. salt
1 c. canned pumpkin
2 c. milk

Mix all ingredients except egg whites. Beat the egg whites until soft peaks form and add to the mix. Pour mix onto oiled, hot waffle iron and cook until golden brown.

HAZELNUT BUTTER

1/2 c. butter, softened
½ tsp. orange peel, grated

1/2 c. hazelnuts, chopped

Mix all ingredients together and top your waffles with this yummy butter!

BREAKFAST

ZIPLOC® OMELET   Pat Magleby

This really works and works well!!! Good for when you have a large crowd for breakfast. Great fun!

Have people write their name on a quart-size Ziploc® freezer bag with a permanent marker. Crack 2 eggs (large or extra-large) into the bag, and shake the bag to combine them.

Put out a variety of ingredients such as: cheeses, ham, onion, green pepper, tomato, hash browns, sliced mushrooms, fresh spinach, salsa, etc. Each guest now adds his or her choice of prepared ingredients to their bag and shakes it again. Make sure to get the air out of the bag and zip it up tight.

Place the bags into rolling, boiling water for 13 to 15 minutes (like you would hard-boil an egg). You can usually cook 6 – 8 omelets in a large pot. For more, make another pot of boiling water. Open the bags. The omelets will roll out easily and everyone will be amazed.

Nice to serve with fresh fruit and coffee cake, and everyone can be involved (reducing the cook's work).

Relief Society Hall, Washington, Utah ~ Constructed in 1875

APPETIZERS & CONDIMENTS

APPETIZERS & CONDIMENTS

ARTICHOKE PARMESAN DIP   Wendy Swanson

1 can artichoke hearts, drained and chopped
1 c. grated parmesan cheese
1 c. Miracle Whip (or mayonnaise if you prefer)
1 clove garlic, minced (optional)

Combine all the ingredients and pour into a shallow casserole dish or glass pie pan. Bake at 350° for about 20 minutes or until bubbly.

Serve with crackers or raw vegetables.

If you'd like a spicier dip, just add a small, well-drained can of chopped green chilies.

APPETIZERS & CONDIMENTS

CHILI CHEESE BITES   Pat Magleby
(Easy Hors d'oeuvre)

4 Tbsp. butter   5 eggs
1/4 c. flour   1/2 tsp. baking powder
Dash of salt   1 4 oz. can chopped green chilies
1 c. small curd cottage cheese   2 c. shredded Monterey Jack cheese

Preheat oven to 400°.

Melt butter in a 9" square pan – tip to cover bottom of pan.

In a large bowl, beat eggs. Stir in flour, baking powder and a dash of salt. Add melted butter.

Stir in chopped green chilies, cottage cheese and Monterey Jack cheese.

Turn batter into butter coated pan and bake for 15 minutes at 400°. Reduce heat to 350° and bake for 30 – 35 minutes longer or until lightly browned.

Cut into squares.

Best served warm – Great served with your favorite salsa.

APPETIZERS & CONDIMENTS

CHILI SAUCE   Wendy Swanson

When I was a child my mother put up all sorts of fruits, vegetables and sauces. She stored it in our crawlspace. It was my job to go down there, fight the spiders and retrieve what she needed. I loved this chili sauce.

2 pan tomatoes
4 large onions
4 large peppers
1 1/2 c. sugar
3 Tbsp. salt
1 c. vinegar
1 tsp. cinnamon
1/2 tsp. black pepper
1/2 tsp. allspice
1/2 tsp. ginger
1/2 tsp. cloves

Let boil until thick; about 2 hours. Bottle like fruit.

What to do with it? Use chili sauce instead of ketchup for an extra zing!

APPETIZERS & CONDIMENTS

CLAM DIP   Joan Silver

This recipe comes from my daughter-in-law Shari Blatter.

2 cans clams, minced (save juice from   2 Tbsp. Worcestershire sauce
   1 can in cup)   2 Tbsp. lemon juice
2 (8 oz.) pkg. cream cheese, softened

Mix all ingredients together and slowly add in the extra clam juice until desired consistency. Serve with potato chips.

DILL WEED VEGETABLE DIP   Joan Silver

This recipe comes from my friend Elga Layton.

2 c. mayo   4 tsp. Bon Appetit
2 c. sour cream   4 tsp. chives
4 tsp. dill weed

Combine all together then chill.   Serve with veggies.

APPETIZERS & CONDIMENTS

FRESH VEGGIE BITES   Wendy Swanson

2 cans crescent rolls
8 oz. pkg. cream cheese, softened
1 pkg. ranch dressing mix
Grated cheese
Chopped bell pepper
Chopped black olives
Grated carrots

Spread rolls on a cookie sheet and bake until light brown. While the rolls are cooling, mix cream cheese and ranch dressing mix. Spread mix on the cooled crusts. Cut the crusts into one or two bite pieces. Top with veggies and cheese. Feel free to add any other vegetables of your choice.

APPETIZERS & CONDIMENTS

HAM SAUCE   Gail Ann Jacobsen

This is a recipe that I received from my Mother-In-Law, Narda Jacobsen. She always made this at Thanksgiving time to serve with the ham. Needless to say, there was always a Turkey and a Ham at our Thanksgiving Feasts! I learned a lot from her and liked the recipes she shared with me.

<u>Mix in a small bowl</u>:
2 eggs lightly beaten   1/2 tsp. salt

<u>Stir into eggs</u>:
2/3 c. sugar   1 Tbsp. flour
1 tsp. dry mustard

<u>Heat</u>: not to boiling…just warmed
2/3 cup vinegar   1/3 cup water

Add egg mixture to heated water and vinegar. Cook to right consistency.

APPETIZERS & CONDIMENTS

JALAPEÑO DIP

Jan Slocum

1 3 ½ oz. can jalapeño peppers (I use about ½ of the can.)
1 4 oz. can green chilies
1 large green pepper (chopped and deseeded)
6 c. sugar
1 c. white vinegar
1 bottle Certo® Liquid Fruit Pectin
Green food coloring

In a blender, blend the jalapeños, chilies and green pepper. Mix with the sugar and vinegar in a large saucepan. Heat to boiling and boil 30 minutes or until skin (film) appears. Add Certo and green food coloring; let set.

Serve with cream cheese on Wheat Thins. Refrigerate any leftovers.

I love this dip because you can make it and it lasts forever. I put it in small containers. You can adjust the heat in the jelly by using more jalapeño peppers.

APPETIZERS & CONDIMENTS

OLIVE DIP   Wendy Swanson

My grandmother's sister, Charlene Musgrave Jones, came up with this recipe about 60 years ago; from then on, my family has been making it. We've always hesitated to share the recipe because it is so simple. It is the easiest dip to make, and everyone will be asking you for the recipe!

8 oz. **softened** cream cheese
1 can (2.25 oz.) chopped black olives

Thoroughly mix the black olives into the softened cream cheese. Serve with potato chips, crackers or use to fill celery sticks. For a softer version that works well for dipping vegetables, substitute the cream cheese with sour cream.

APPETIZERS & CONDIMENTS

MUSTARD SAUCE   Norma Dooley
(from Sweden)

This recipe was given to me by Marva Nelson in Sun River. This sauce was served with ham at the lunch after the funeral for Merle Rust.

1 1/2 c. granulated sugar   2 heaping Tbsp. flour
1 tsp. salt
1 rounded Tbsp. Colman's dry mustard. (It must be Colman's)

Mix ingredients with whisk, then stir in:

4 eggs

Whisk again. Add:

1 c. water   1 c. white vinegar

Stir with whisk to mix well.

Cook in microwave 3 minutes. Stir well. Cook for 1 minute and stir. Cook till thick, repeating 3 times; stirring well after each minute. Makes 1 quart. Refrigerate in glass jar.

This sauce will keep for a long time. It is good on sandwiches instead of mayo.

This mustard sauce is a must with ham. It is sooooo good. We sometimes run out of this sauce before the ham is gone.

COLESLAW DRESSING   Norma Dooley

1 Tbsp. mustard sauce*
1 Tbsp. mayo

*See mustard sauce recipe on previous page.

Stir with whisk to mix well.

APPETIZERS & CONDIMENTS

SPICE RUB   Gail Ann Jacobsen

This recipe can be used with the meat of your choice. You only need a little. Helps spice up the meat, especially "chicken".

1 Tbsp. smoked paprika   2 Tbsp. garlic powder
2 tsp. onion powder   1/2 tsp. black pepper
2 tsp. chili powder   2 tsp. ground cumin
1/2 tsp. cayenne   1 Tbsp. dried chives
1 Tbsp. Splenda® Brown Sugar Blend   1 tsp. kosher salt
1 Packet Splenda® or Stevia

Suggestions for using the Spice Rub:

1. Rub on chicken or your desired meat; place it in the crock pot for about 4 hours. Ready for the rest of the planned meal.

2. Place your desired meat, after you have applied the rub and cut it into squares, so it cooks quickly, on a pan with parchment paper. Cut up different veggies, like zucchini, cauliflower, broccoli, asparagus, bell peppers or anything that you like to roast.

3. Bake the whole pan @ 400° for about 20 minutes with meat on one side of the pan and the veggies on the other side (with no rub).

Store any unused portion in a glass covered dish in a cool, dry place.

APPETIZERS & CONDIMENTS

ROASTED RED PEPPER HUMMUS   Wendy Swanson

1 can chickpeas, rinsed
1 clove garlic, crushed
1/4 c. olive oil
1/4 c. roasted red peppers
2 Tbsp. fresh lemon juice
2 drops sesame oil (optional)
1 tsp. ground cumin
1/4 tsp. paprika
Salt

In a food processor, blend the chickpeas and garlic with the olive oil, lemon juice, sesame oil (if using), cumin, and 3/4 tsp. salt until smooth. Add the peppers to the hummus and process until smooth and creamy. Add 1 to 2 tablespoons water as necessary to achieve the proper consistency.

Pour hummus into a bowl. Drizzle with olive oil and sprinkle with the paprika before serving. Serve with pita chips or raw veggies.

SOUPS & STEWS

SOUPS & STEWS

BEST EVER BEEF STEW   Joan Silver

2 lbs. beef stew meat

1/2 c. all-purpose flour

1 Tbsp. seasoning salt

2 Tbsp. olive oil

1/2 tsp. black pepper

1 large onion, diced

2 bay leaves

1/4 c. Worcestershire sauce

2 c. water

2 heaping tsp. beef demi-glace or beef Swanson Flavor Boost or
    Better than Bouillon

4 medium to large red skinned potatoes, washed & diced

3 large carrots, peeled & sliced

1 stalk celery, diced

Shake the beef stew meat in a resealable plastic bag with the flour and seasoning salt until evenly coated. Heat the olive oil in a skillet; add the floured stew meat to the pan and brown on all sides. Remove, using a slotted spoon or tongs and place into the bottom of a slow cooker. Season with pepper.

Sauté the diced onion in the same hot skillet for 2 minutes. Don't worry about cleaning it out in between – that's added flavor! Transfer the onions into the slow cooker as well. Pour the Worcestershire sauce, water and beef demi-glace (or Swanson Flavor Boost or Better than Bouillon) into the skillet and whisk until mixed; making sure you scrape up any browned bits in the bottom of the pan. Turn off the heat and set aside.

Add the diced potatoes, carrots, celery and bay leaves to the slow cooker. Now, pour the broth/Worcestershire mixture into the crock pot as well. Cover; cook on low for 8 hours. Remove the bay leaves before serving.

SOUPS & STEWS

BRATTEN'S CLAM CHOWDER   Joan Silver

3/4 c. butter
3/4 c. flour
1 pt. whipping cream
4 tsp. sugar
2 c. red or new white potatoes, diced with skin on

1 c. celery, diced
1/2 c. onion, diced
2 cans clams, chopped or minced
1 1/2 tsp. salt

Place potatoes, celery and onion in a large heavy soup pan, cover with water; add a little salt and pepper and bring them to a boil. Cook until tender. I like to remove my potatoes with a slotted spoon and set them aside in a separate bowl. (This is so they don't get mashed up while making the sauce.) Add the sugar, the rest of the salt, and cream to the water you cooked the vegetables in.

In a separate pan, make your roux by melting the butter first then adding the flour. Mix until it is smooth and not lumpy. Add the roux to the cream mixture in the large soup pan. Cook on medium high heat stirring constantly until it thickens. You may need to add some more liquid if it is too thick. Use the juice from the clams first, and if you need more, use milk. If it needs to be thicker, then make some more roux and add it in and continue to cook and stir on medium until it is how you like it. Add in the clams and cooked potatoes and serve.

SOUPS & STEWS

BROCCOLI–CHEESE SOUP
Wendy Swanson

32 oz. frozen, chopped broccoli

2 cans (10 3/4 oz.) Campbell's® condensed cheddar cheese soup

2 cans evaporated milk

1/4 c. dried minced onion

1/2 tsp. salt

1/4 tsp. pepper

Combine all ingredients in a greased 4 to 6-quart slow cooker. Cover and cook on high heat for 2-3 hours or on low heat 4-5 hours.

Garnish with crumbled bacon.

SOUPS & STEWS

CROCK POT CHILI   Wendy Swanson

2 lbs. ground beef, browned and drained
1 large onion, chopped or 1/2 c. dried minced onion
1 large can (28 oz.) diced tomatoes, with liquid
2 (8 oz.) cans tomato purée
1 (16 oz.) can kidney beans, with liquid
1 can (4 oz.) diced green chilies, with liquid
1 c. water
2 Tbsp. chili powder
2 tsp. salt
1 tsp. pepper
Bread bowls

Combine all ingredients in a greased 4 to 6 quart slow cooker. Cover and cook on high heat for 2-3 hours or on low heat 4-6 hours. Serve in bread bowls.

Garnish with sour cream, chives and grated cheese.

SOUPS & STEWS

EASY SOUP   Gail Ann Jacobsen

1 family size can chicken and rice soup
1 can corn, not drained
1 can Rotell tomatoes w/cilantro (you can use any kind of tomatoes, if the Rotell tomatoes are too spicy)
1 can ranch style beans
Cooked chicken, chopped into small pieces. (I use a rotisserie chicken that I de-bone and chopped, using as much as I wanted in the soup.)

Add all ingredients together and add however much water you would like to make it the consistency your family likes. Heat in a large saucepan.

Serve with grated cheese and chips.

SOUPS & STEWS

GRANDPA'S SOUP   Maxine Humphrey

1 large can Pork 'n' Beans
1 large can Progresso® Minestrone Soup
1 lb. lean ground beef
1 c. whole tomatoes
Chopped onions

Place ingredients in crock pot. Cover and cook on low for several hours.

SOUPS & STEWS

HEARTY HODGEPODGE SOUP   Joan Silver

1 1/2 lbs. ground beef
3/4 c. onion, chopped
1 tsp. garlic powder
3 cans condensed Minestrone soup
3 c. water

1 (13 oz.) can pork and beans
1 1/2 c. celery chopped
1 Tbsp. Worcestershire sauce
1/2 tsp. oregano

In a large pan, cook the beef, onion and garlic until the beef is browned and the onion is tender. Stir in remaining ingredients and simmer, covered for 15 to 20 minutes.

Serve with crackers or breadsticks.

This is so good and easy to make.

SOUPS & STEWS

MACARONI AND TOMATO SOUP   Maxine Humphrey

2 Tbsp. margarine
1/2 c. chopped onions
1/4 c. diced green pepper
1 c. diced celery
1 c. tomato soup
1 c. water
1 c. tomato juice
4 oz. macaroni, cooked
Dash of pepper
1/2 tsp. salt
1/2 tsp. sweet basil
1 Tbsp. sugar
1 or 2 bay leaves

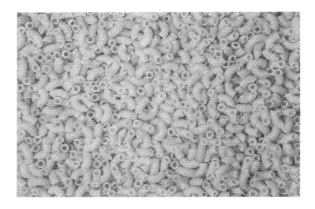

In heavy saucepan, melt butter and cook onion, green pepper and celery until limp, but not brown. Add remaining ingredients and heat to boiling.

SOUPS & STEWS

PIONEER BEAN SOUP   Maxine Humphrey

1 pt. bean soup mix
7 c. water
1 ham hock
1 clove garlic, minced
1 onion, chopped
1 tsp. chili powder
1 or 2 tsp. salt
1 – 8 oz. can tomato sauce
2 carrots, chopped
1 celery stalk, chopped

Place ingredients in crock pot. Cover and cook over medium for 7 hours or until beans are tender.

Remove meat from ham hock and return to the soup.

Before serving, add the juice from one lemon to the soup and top with grated cheese and sour cream.

SOUPS & STEWS

POTATO SOUP

Gail Ann Jacobsen

1 (30 oz.) bag frozen hash-brown potatoes (I use the squared, southern style)
2 (14 oz.) cans chicken broth
1 (10.75 oz.) can cream of chicken soup (or S.OS. mix)
In a slow cooker, combine potatoes, broth, soup, onion and pepper. Cover and cook on low for 5 hours.

Stir in Greek yogurt; cook 30 minutes, stirring occasionally, until combined. Garnish with green onion.

I topped with shredded cheese and bacon bits, because I had them on hand. Otherwise, I followed the recipe exactly. You could even have a "toppings bar" at your party, letting your guests choose from all sorts of toppings for their soup...Shredded cheese, chives, bacon bits, sour cream, etc. Then serve with crackers or bread.

SOUPS & STEWS

PRINT SHOP SOUP   Joan Silver

3 carrots
1 yellow onion
1 sm. Celery head (3 -5 stalks)
3 cubes of real butter (3/4 lb.)
1 1/2 c. flour (for roux)
1 cheese whiz (1 lb.)
1 1/2 gallons water
6 oz. chicken broth
frozen peas

Slice and dice veggies. Cook in chicken broth until crisp tender. Melt butter and mix with flour to make a roux. Blend in slowly with broth. Add cheese whiz. Simmer. Add peas. Heat through.

SOUPS & STEWS

TACO SOUP   Maxine Humphrey

Western Family tomato juice (or use vegetable cocktail juice instead)
1 lb. hamburger
diced onion
1 pkg. mild taco seasoning
1 can corn, drained
2 cans kidney beans
1 can Pork 'n' Beans
1 can pinto beans

Brown the hamburger and diced onion; drain the grease. Place all ingredients in a crock pot. Cover and cook on low for several hours.

Crumble corn chips on top before serving.

SOUPS & STEWS

URBAN COWBOY SOUP   Wendy Swanson

1 medium onion
1 can diced tomatoes with green chilies
1 can stewed tomatoes
1 can of black beans or pinto beans, drained
1 (15 oz.) can whole kernel corn, drained
1 or 2 bell peppers, chopped
1 box Spanish or Mexican style rice with seasoning packet
1 c. diced celery
1 3/4 c. vegetable bouillon
6 oz. *Gia's Cheesorizo Fiesta (cheese sausage) or chorizo

Combine all ingredients in a greased 4 to 6 quart slow cooker. Cover and cook on low heat for 4 to 5 hours. Don't overcook.

Top with grated cheese and serve with homemade bread or tortilla chips.

*If your grocery store doesn't carry Gia's Cheesorizo you can purchase it direct at cheesorizo.com.

SOUPS & STEWS

WHITE CHICKEN CHILI SOUP   Tamara Rogers

4 c. chicken broth
4 – 15.5 oz. cans Great Northern beans, drained and rinsed
2 c. shredded chicken
1 small can diced green chilies
1 tsp. cumin
1/2 tsp. garlic powder
1/2 tsp. oregano
1/2 tsp. pepper
1 c. sour cream
2 c. shredded cheese, Monterrey Jack or Mexican Blend

In a large pot; add broth, beans, chicken, green chilies, cumin, garlic powder, oregano and pepper. Simmer on low-medium heat for 20-30 minutes, or until it is heated through.

Right before serving, stir in sour cream and cheese until it is all blended and melted.

SALADS & SIDE DISHES

SALADS & SIDE DISHES

AMBROSIA SALAD   Wendy Swanson

8 oz. Cool Whip, thawed
3/4 c. maraschino cherries,
    sliced in half, stems removed
1 c. fresh pineapple chunks
3/4 c. chopped pecans

1/2 c. sour cream
1 (15 oz.) can mandarin oranges,
    drained
3 c. mini marshmallows

In a large bowl, combine Cool Whip and sour cream until well mixed. Gently stir in the maraschino cherries, mandarin oranges, pineapple chunks, mini marshmallows and chopped pecans until combined.

Chill for at least one hour before serving. This is a salad that can be made the night before.

SALADS & SIDE DISHES

AVOCADO STRAWBERRY SPINACH SALAD   Gail Ann Jacobsen
with POPPY SEED DRESSING

Salad:

6 c. fresh baby spinach, no stems

1 avocado, diced (or you can double this to 2 avocados)

1/4 c. sliced almonds, toasted

1 pint strawberries, hulled and sliced

4 oz. crumbled gorgonzola or blue cheese

half a small red onion, thinly sliced

Poppy Seed Dressing Ingredients:

1/2 c. oil

2 Tbsp. honey

pinch of ground dry mustard (optional)

3 Tbsp. apple cider vinegar

1 Tbsp. poppy seeds

salt and pepper

Wisk all ingredients together until combined. Toss all ingredients together with desired amount of dressing until combined. Serve immediately.

SALADS & SIDE DISHES

CHICKEN BOW TIE PASTA SALAD   Joan Silver

3 pkg. bow tie pasta
  (multi colored–opt.)
4 chicken breasts, cooked and cubed
2 bunches of green onions, chopped

10 -11 celery stalks, diced
1 pkg. slivered almonds
2 lrg. cans pineapple tidbits, drained
grapes, sliced in half

Cook pasta as directed on box. Drain. Combine all ingredients and set aside.

Dressing:

2 (16 oz.) bottles Hidden Valley®
  coleslaw dressing
pineapple juice from tidbits

1 (32 oz.) jar mayo

Combine dressing and mayo. Thin with pineapple juice if needed. Pour over salad and mix in.

SALADS & SIDE DISHES

CHRISTMAS RIBBON SALAD   Wendy Swanson

My dad, Jerry Warren makes this salad every year at Christmastime. This is the only time he does any food preparation except when we used to go camping.

2 pkg. lime gelatin
1 pkg. lemon gelatin
1 c. boiling water
1 can (8 oz.) crushed pineapple,
   drained

1 8 oz. pkg. cream cheese
2 c. whipped topping
2 pkg. cherry gelatin
1/4 c. chopped pecans

Prepare lime gelatin according to directions. Pour into a 13x9" dish, coated with cooking spray. Chill until almost set, about 2 hours. Dissolve lemon gelatin in 1 c. boiling water. Whisk in cream cheese until smooth. Stir in pineapple and pecans. Fold in whipped topping. Chill until almost set, about 1 hour. Carefully pour over lime gelatin and return to refrigerator. Prepare cherry gelatin according to package directions. Chill until consistency of egg whites. Carefully pour over pineapple layer. Chill until firm.

Tip: Dissolve gelatin in a bottle by shaking it. It's quicker and won't make a mess.

SALADS & SIDE DISHES

CITRUS SALAD TOSS   Gail Ann Jacobsen

Ingredients:

2/3 c. sugared pecans

8 c. torn Romaine lettuce

1 large orange, peeled and sliced
   (mandarin oranges can be
   substituted)

8 c. torn leaf lettuce

1 red onion, thinly sliced

1 pint strawberries cut into halves

2 avocadoes, thinly sliced

Combine the lettuce, onion, oranges and strawberries in a large salad bowl and toss gently. Add the avocadoes just before serving. Drizzle with the dressing, tossing gently. Top with the pecans.

Dressing:

2/3 c. vegetable oil

2 Tbsp. orange juice

1 tsp. grated lime zest

1/4 c. lime juice

2 Tbsp. sugar

1 tsp. grated orange zest

Combine the oil, lime juice, orange juice, sugar, lime zest and orange zest in an airtight jar and shake well. Chill until serving time.

SALADS & SIDE DISHES

CURRIED CHICKEN SALAD WRAPS   Gail Ann Jacobsen

1 10-oz. can of chicken breast packed in water
1/2 c. low-fat plain Greek yogurt
1/2 tsp. curry powder
1/2 c. diced celery
2 Tbsp. fresh parsley, chopped
1/4 tsp. salt
1/4 tsp. ground pepper
8 large green leaf or romaine lettuce leaves
2/3 oz. chopped peanuts

Mix the chicken, yogurt, celery herbs and spices together in a medium bowl.

Prepare wraps by topping lettuce leaves with chicken salad, sprinkling with peanuts, and rolling wraps.

Makes 2 servings.

SALADS & SIDE DISHES

DIXIE SALAD   Maxine Humphrey

2 c. pomegranate seeds
1 can pineapple tidbits, drained
4 bananas, peeled and sliced
3 c. tart apples, peeled, cored and chopped
1/2 c. pecans, chopped
3 Tbsp. Mayonnaise
2 Tbsp. creamy salad dressing

In a large bowl, combine the pomegranate seeds, pineapple, bananas, apples and pecans.

Stir in the mayo and salad dressing until evenly coated.

Cover and refrigerate overnight before serving.

SALADS & SIDE DISHES

SWEET DIXIE SALAD   Wendy Swanson

A friend of mine, Loreena Pedersen, gave me this recipe when I lived in southern Oregon. She was born and raised in southern Utah. She said traditionally, this recipe only contained ingredients that were grown here in Dixie.

1 c. pomegranate arils
2 c. chopped, firm apple
1 c. chopped pecans
1 c. whipping cream
3 Tbsp. sugar
1 tsp. vanilla

In a small bowl, whip the cream with sugar and vanilla until stiff peaks appear.

In a large bowl, add the pomegranate arils, apples and pecans. (Feel free to add any other fruit you would like.) Gently fold in the whipped cream and garnish with a few pomegranate arils. Serve right away.

Store any leftovers in a covered container in the fridge for up to a day.

SALADS & SIDE DISHES

EASY OVEN BROWN RICE   Tamara Rogers

1 1/2 c. brown rice
2 Tbsp. butter
1 tsp. salt
3 c. boiling water

Preheat oven to 400°.

Place rice, salt and butter in a casserole dish that has a cover. Pour boiling water over rice; stir.

Cover and bake in a preheated oven until liquid is absorbed and rice is tender; about 1 hour. Remove from oven, fluff with fork and serve hot.

SALADS & SIDE DISHES

FRIED CABBAGE   Judy Call

When I first tasted this, I thought it was mashed potatoes. I couldn't believe it was cabbage! This really is a pioneer recipe. It never was written down, just word of mouth.

8 slices bacon, chopped	1 c. onion, chopped
1 large head of cabbage, cored and chopped fine	1 egg, whipped
Salt and pepper, added for taste	Option – dash of garlic powder

Cook the bacon in a jumbo cooker over medium-high heat until crisp. Remove the bacon to a paper towel-lined plate. Reserve 2 teaspoons of the bacon grease and discard the rest. In the same jumbo cooker, return the 2 teaspoons of bacon grease. Over medium-high heat cook the onion until it is soft; about 4 minutes. Stir in the cabbage and continue to cook and stir for 4 – 5 minutes. Add the seasonings; salt, pepper and garlic powder if desired. Mix well.

Reduce heat to low, add beaten egg well into cabbage mixture; cover and allow to simmer; stirring occasionally for about 30 minutes or until egg mixture is cooked.

Just before serving, mix the bacon back into the cooked cabbage mixture. Serve immediately.

SALADS & SIDE DISHES

FROG EYE SALAD   Marlene Mason Wood

This recipe was given to me by my mother, Roa Dean Shaw Mason. A family favorite.

1 c. granulated sugar
2 Tbsp. flour
2 eggs, beaten
1 Tbsp. lemon juice
1 pkg. Acini de pepe pasta
  (very small, round pasta)

1 can pineapple chunks (lrg. can)
3 cans mandarin oranges
1 (8 oz.) container Cool Whip
1 c. miniature marshmallows
1 Tbsp. cooking oil
2 1/2 c. pineapple juice
1/2 tsp. salt

Combine sugar, flour and salt. Drain pineapple to get juice (if there isn't enough juice, add water). Stir into flour mixture and add eggs. Cook on medium heat until thickened. Add lemon juice and let cool. Bring 3 quarts of water to boil. Add salt and oil. Cook noodles for 8 minutes. Drain, rinse and cool. Add other mixture to noodles and let refrigerate overnight. Next day add fruit, Cool Whip and marshmallows.

SALADS & SIDE DISHES

FUNERAL POTATOES   Wendy Swanson

This recipe was given to me by a friend. She had prepared them for a lunch held after the funeral of one of our friends. She told me they are called "funeral potatoes" because they are a basic menu item served after most LDS funerals.

2 lbs. hash browns
2 (10 ¾ oz) cans condensed cream of chicken soup
3/4 c. chopped onion
2 c. Colby cheese, shredded and firmly packed

1/2 c. butter
1 pint sour cream
1/2 tsp. salt
1 Tbsp. butter
1 1/2 c. crushed corn flakes
4 Tbsp. melted butter

Sauté the onion in 1 tablespoon of butter until clear. Mix all ingredients except corn flakes and 4 tablespoons together. Pour potato mixture into a 9x13 glass casserole dish (or baking pan). In a bowl, combine cornflakes and 4 tablespoons of melted butter. Sprinkle corn flake mixture evenly over potato mixture.

Bake in a to 350° oven for 40 to 50 minutes until bubbly.

SALADS & SIDE DISHES

GARLIC MASHED SWEET POTATOES
Gail Ann Jacobsen

2 lbs. (4 medium) sweet potatoes, peeled and cubed
1 Tbsp. butter
3 cloves garlic, crushed
1/2 c. 1% milk
2 Tbsp. light sour cream
Salt and fresh cracked pepper to taste

In a large pot boil sweet potatoes in salted water until tender, drain in a colander.

Meanwhile, melt butter and sauté garlic until lightly golden. Return potatoes to the pan.

Add milk and sour cream; mash until smooth and creamy. Adjust salt and pepper to taste.

Serving size: 3/4 cup.

SALADS & SIDE DISHES

GRANDMA ROA'S JELLO   Marlene Mason Wood

This recipe was given to me by my mother, Roa Dean Shaw Mason. Another family favorite.

1 large container Cool Whip, unfrozen
1 can Eagle Brand Sweetened Condensed Milk

1 can of pie filling, any kind
1 can crushed pineapple, drained
1/2 pkg. mini marshmallows

Combine and mix all ingredients together. Pour into glass bowl or glass tray. Place in refrigerator overnight to firm. Serve. Yummy!

SALADS & SIDE DISHES

GREEN JELLO SALAD   Wendy Swanson

Green Jello Salad has been called the "official snack of Utah" and was featured on a 2002 Olympics collectible pin.

1 box lime Jello (3 oz. box)
1 c. shredded carrots
1 c. crushed pineapple (save the juice)
1 c. water

Place the shredded carrots in the bottom of an 8x8 glass dish. Drain the crushed pineapple and save the juice in a measuring cup. Add enough ice cubes to the juice to equal one cup.

Spread the crushed pineapple over the shredded carrots.

In the microwave, heat the 1 cup of water. In a bowl, add the water to the Jello and stir until dissolved. Add the pineapple juice/ice mixture until the ice has melted.

Pour the Jello mixture over the carrots and pineapple. Refrigerate until firm (for at least two hours) before serving.

SALADS & SIDE DISHES

KFC® COLESLAW   Gail Ann Jacobsen

This is the coleslaw that my family likes the very best. I was excited to find this recipe and even more excited when I followed the recipe. I hope that you will like it also.

1/2 c. mayonnaise
1/3 c. sugar
1/4 c. milk
1/4 c. buttermilk
2 1/2 Tbsp. lemon juice
1 1/2 Tbsp. white vinegar
1/2 tsp. salt
1/8 t. pepper
8 c. finely chopped cabbage
1/4 c. shredded carrots (I chop the shredded carrots
   with a chopper)
2 tsp. minced onion

Chop the veggies fine. Combine mayonnaise, milk, buttermilk, lemon juice, and vinegar. Add in sugar, salt and pepper. Beat until smooth. Add cabbage, carrots and onion. Mix well. Chill at least 2 hours.

SALADS & SIDE DISHES

MACARONI SALAD   Marlene Mason Wood

This recipe was given to me by my mother, Roa Dean Shaw Mason. Our family loved picnicking and going to the mountains. We liked taking this salad with us, with chicken. Those were special memories!

1 c. real mayonnaise
2 Tbsp. vinegar
1 tsp. sugar
1 tsp. salt
1/4 tsp. pepper
8 oz. elbow macaroni, cooked and drained (makes 2 cups cooked)
1 c. celery, diced
1 c. green pepper, diced
1/4 c. chopped onions
1 small pkg. frozen peas
1 can of ham or shrimp

In a large bowl, stir together the first six ingredients until smooth. Add remaining ingredients, toss to coat well. Cover and chill. Makes 5 cups.

SALADS & SIDE DISHES

NO GREEN BEANS SALAD   Wendy Swanson

Traditional bean salad has green beans and wax beans, but I don't care for either one, so this is my version of bean salad.

1 can garbanzo beans	1 can kidney beans
1 can cannellini beans	1/2 red onion, chopped
1/4 bell pepper, any color	2 celery stalks, finely chopped
3/4 c. sugar	3/4 c. vinegar
1 tsp. salt	1/2 c. oil

Drain liquid from beans. Add onion, pepper and celery. Mix together sugar, vinegar, salt and oil. Add to bean mixture. Marinate in the refrigerator for at least 8 hours.

Tip: Put onions in a plastic bag in the crisper. Then when you peel them, they won't make you cry.

SALADS & SIDE DISHES

NORMA STAY'S SUNSHINE SALAD   Maxine Humphrey

Norma Stay was a stalwart member of Mulberry Camp. She wrote the Mulberry Camp song featured on the front page of our booklet this past year. We sing this song at the beginning of every camp meeting.

This is her recipe for Sunshine Salad which is a favorite at our house. I always think of Norma when I fix it. Those of us who knew her and worked with her love and miss her. It is only fitting that one of her favorite recipes be in our recipe book.

Filling:
1 large cooked lemon pudding (following the package directions)
1 small orange jello pkg.
2 c. boiling water

Add jello and boiling water to cooked pudding. Pour into a baking dish. Chill overnight.

Topping:
1 small pkg. instant lemon pudding
1 c. milk
1 1/2 c. Cool Whip
Mandarin oranges

Combine pudding with milk and stir in Cool Whip. Spread on top of the chilled pudding/jello mix and then line with mandarin oranges.

PISTACHIO SALAD   Joan Silver

1 (6 oz.) box instant pistachio
  pudding
1 (20 oz.) can crushed pineapple,
  drained

1 (9 oz.) carton whipped topping
  (Cool Whip)
2 c. miniature marshmallows
1/2 c. chopped pistachios (opt.)

Mix all ingredients together. Chill before serving

SALADS & SIDE DISHES

ROASTED ASPARAGUS   Norma Dooley

Trim asparagus. Cut into bite size pieces or leave in long spears.

Put in bowl and drizzle with olive oil. Toss to mix.

Spread on cookie sheet covered with foil and sprayed with nonstick spray. Keep in one layer.

Sprinkle on seasons you like; garlic powder, salt, lemon pepper, parmesan cheese.

Heat oven to 400°. Bake for 20 minutes.

Any vegetable can be roasted this way. We especially like cauliflower and baby carrots, and of course asparagus roasted this way.

SALADS & SIDE DISHES

PASTA SALAD   Maxine Humphrey

1 lb. mushrooms, sliced
1/2 red pepper, sliced
1/2 green pepper, sliced

Marinate vegetables overnight with a large bottle of Wishbone® Italian dressing and 1/2 bottle of McCormick® Salad Supreme seasoning.

The next day add:

3 medium chopped tomatoes
1 lb. cubed Mozzarella cheese
1 c. medium olives
1 lb. chicken or crab
Imitation pepperoni
1 pkg. colored cork screw noodles, cooked.

Refrigerate for 2 to 3 hours before serving.

SALADS & SIDE DISHES

SKINNY BROCCOLI SALAD   Gail Ann Jacobsen

3 c. broccoli florets
1/4 c. Fage plain Greek yogurt
3 Tbsp. reduced fat mayo
2 packets Stevia or sweetener of choice
1 Tbsp. apple cider vinegar
1/4 tsp. salt, optional
2 Tbsp. low sodium real bacon bits
1 oz. sliced almonds
1/3 c. reduced fat shredded cheddar cheese

Place washed broccoli florets in a medium sized bowl, set aside.

In a small bowl combine yogurt, mayo, sweetener, vinegar and salt. Stir until smooth. Pour yogurt mixture over broccoli and stir until all combined.

Add sliced almonds, bacon and cheese. Toss gently until all pieces are evenly coated.

SALADS & SIDE DISHES

SOUTHWEST CHOPPED SALAD   Wendy Swanson

Large head of romaine lettuce, 15 oz.
1 can of black beans, rinsed and drained
1 large orange or red bell pepper
1 pint cherry tomatoes
2 c. corn (fresh or frozen, thawed)
5 green onions
Hidden Valley® southwest chipotle dressing
Broken tortilla chips

Finely chop romaine, bell pepper, tomatoes, and green onions. Place all ingredients, except dressing and tortilla chips in a large bowl and stir to combine. Just before serving toss with dressing and top with broken tortilla chips

SALADS & SIDE DISHES

TACO SALAD   Maxine Humphrey

1 lb. browned hamburger
1 head lettuce
1 pkg. taco seasoning
1 c. black olives
1 lb. shredded cheese
2 chopped tomatoes
1 can red kidney beans
1 pkg. Doritos®

Gently toss all ingredients together, except the Doritos®.

Add the Doritos® on top and then garnish with salsa, sour cream and Ranch dressing.

SALADS & SIDE DISHES

THREE BEAN SALAD   Joan Silver

1 can French cut green beans   1 can red kidney beans
1 can yellow wax beans   1 can garbanzo beans (optional)

Drain cans well. Pour into a large bowl.

½ c. green peppers, minced   3/4 c. brown sugar
1/2 c. minced onion   1 tsp. salt
1/2 c. salad oil   1/2 tsp. pepper
1/2 c. cider vinegar

Add the green pepper and onion to the beans.

Stir together and toss with the above mixture: oil, cider vinegar, sugar, salt and pepper.

Let sit overnight.

SALADS & SIDE DISHES

SUNSHINE SALAD   Gail Ann Jacobsen

1/4 c. yellow bell pepper
1/4 c. cucumber
6 oz. grilled chicken
1/2 c. feta cheese, crumbled
Toasted almonds, as many as you
   desire

1/4 c. yellow tomatoes
1/4 c. jicama
1 c. red leaf lettuce
1 Tbsp. lemon zest
Fresh basil leaves (approx. 4 for a
   large salad, diced)

The veggies and chicken should be cut into bite-sized pieces or sliced. Toss all ingredients together.

The ingredients above make a serving for **one** and just a good suggestion. You can multiply it for more than one serving, and add to it, to your own taste.

Serve with the Homemade Lemon Vinaigrette.
(Recipe is on the following page.)

SALADS & SIDE DISHES

HOMEMADE LEMON VINAIGRETTE   Gail Ann Jacobsen

1/3 c. olive oil
1/4 c. lemon juice
2 tsp. Walden Farms pancake syrup or sugar free syrup.
1 tsp. Dijon mustard
1 small garlic clove minced

In a small bowl, whisk together all the ingredients.

Store the dressing in the fridge. Shake well before using.

SALADS & SIDE DISHES

TWICE BAKED SWEET POTATOES   Wendy Swanson

5 medium sized sweet potatoes	2 Tbsp. butter
1/2 c. cranberry relish	1/2 tsp. salt
1/2 c. dried cranberries or raisins	1/2 c. walnut or pecan pieces

Scrub sweet potatoes and pierce all over with a fork. Place them in a preheated 325° oven for 1 hour or until tender.

After cooling enough to handle, slice each one lengthwise. Scoop the pulp out, and place in a medium sized bowl. Mash the potatoes with a fork or potato masher (do not whip them). Stir in cranberry relish, cranberries or raisins, butter and salt.

Spoon potato mixture back into their skins and place on a cookie sheet. Sprinkle with the walnuts or pecan pieces.

Bake in a 375° oven for 15 minutes or until heated through.

BREADS & ROLLS

BREADS & ROLLS

ARTISAN BREAD   Tamara Rogers

3 c. white flour	1 tsp. salt
1/2 tsp. yeast	1 1/2 c. warm water

You'll start by mixing the flour, salt, yeast and warm water in a bowl.

Use a wooden spoon and just mix until everything's combined; probably less than a minute. No kneading and no worries if it looks like a shaggy mess. It's ok.

Cover with plastic wrap and leave at room temperature for 8-24 hours. It will get all bubbly.

About 90 minutes before you'd like to serve it, turn the dough out onto a **well-floured** surface. Form it into a ball and let is rest for 30 minutes.

In the meantime, turn on the oven to 450° and put whatever dish you'll cook it in inside the oven to preheat. You can use a Dutch oven, or the crock from your slow-cooker* (that's what I use), or a casserole dish with high sides, or an oven safe pot…pretty much anything that's oven safe and has high sides will work.

After the dough has rested and the oven has preheated 30 minutes, use a sharp knife to slash an X across the top of the dough. Spray your baking dish with nonstick spray, pick up the dough with floured hands and plop it in. Cover the dish with a lid or aluminum foil and put it in the oven.

Bake covered for 30 minutes, then uncover and bake 10-15 minutes more until top is nicely browned.

I like to let the bread cool for **at least** 15 minutes before I slice it, so it doesn't squish. If you have an electric knife you may be able to cut it sooner; and if you don't have a sharp, serrated knife, you might want to wait even longer. It'll be worth it; I promise!

I've heard that a crock can crack from the heat in the oven. I have used mine multiple times and it has been fine, but I'd hate for anyone to ruin their crock on my advice! So, use a crock at your own risk.

BREADS & ROLLS

BEAN-O-NUTS (BEAN DOUGHNUTS)   Judy Call

3 c. unsifted flour
3 tsp. baking powder
1/2 tsp. nutmeg
1 1/4 c. sugar
1 c. milk

1/2 tsp. salt
1/2 tsp. cinnamon
2 Tbsp. shortening
2 eggs, well beaten
1 tsp. vanilla

1 c. cooked, cold, unseasoned pinto beans; mashed (I use the canned pinto beans)

Sift flour with salt, baking powder and spices; set aside. In a large mixing bowl, beat shortening and sugar. Add eggs and beat until very light and fluffy - about two minutes. Add pinto beans and vanilla. Add half the dry ingredients along with the milk, and then add the rest of the dry ingredients.

Chill dough. Turn onto a lightly floured board. Roll 1/4 inch thick, cut with floured donut cutter. Fry in deep fat 385°. Drain on absorbent paper. Makes 2 dozen. Sprinkle while warm with cinnamon sugar mixture of 1 cup granulated sugar and 1 teaspoon cinnamon.

This is amazing and fun to do with children and grandchildren. One way to get them to eat their beans.

BREADS & ROLLS

BREADSTICKS   Tamara Rogers

Melt about 1/3 c. butter in a cookie sheet.

Stir together:

2 1/4 c. flour	3 1/2 tsp. baking powder
1 Tbsp. sugar	1 1/2 tsp. salt

Add 1 c. milk.

Stir with fork; then turn onto a well-floured board. Knead lightly; about 10 times.

Roll out the dough same size as the cookie sheet. Use a pizza cutter to cut once lengthwise, then crosswise to the width you desire. Dip each piece in butter on both sides and lay close together.

Bake in a 425° oven about 10-15 minutes.

You can add ½ c. grated sharp cheese to dry ingredients or sprinkle with cinnamon and sugar.

BREADS & ROLLS

CAKE DOUGHNUTS   Wendy Swanson

As a child, I always looked forward to my mom, Dixie Burke Warren, making these doughnuts. She used a deep pan of hot oil, but it's easier to use a deep fryer.

1 c. sugar	1 tsp. salt
5 Tbsp. shortening	1 c. milk
3 eggs, beaten	1 tsp. nutmeg
4 tsp. baking powder	4 1/2 - 5 c. sifted flour

Cream shortening and sugar; add eggs and beat well. Add milk and flour sifted with salt, baking powder and nutmeg alternately to the mixture. Add enough flour to make soft dough. Roll on lightly floured surface and cut out with floured doughnut cutter. Fry in a deep fryer until dough turns golden brown.

BREADS & ROLLS

CINNAMON ROLLS
Wendy Swanson

This is a recipe I got from my mom, Dixie Burke Warren. It was always a special treat to get home from school on a cold winter day and find that she'd made these wonderful rolls.

4 pkg. yeast	1 c. water
4 c. scalded milk	8 Tbsp. shortening
8 Tbsp. sugar	4 tsp. salt
4 well beaten eggs	12 c. flour

Soften yeast in warm water. Combine milk, shortening, sugar and salt. Add yeast and eggs. Gradually stir in flour to form soft dough. Beat vigorously. Cover and let double. Divide dough in thirds. Roll out on a floured surface. Spread melted butter, sugar and cinnamon on dough (you can add raisins if you like). Roll lengthwise and seal edges. Put in a pan and let rise double. Slice into rolls. Bake at 375° for about 25 minutes.

Frost with a powdered sugar icing. Stir 2 Tbsp. milk into 1 c. powdered sugar, then add 1/2 tsp. clear vanilla. You can add a little more milk or powdered sugar until the icing is the consistency you want.

BREADS & ROLLS

CARDAMOM BRAID
Wendy Swanson

My mom loves the flavor of cardamom; so Mom, this recipe is for you.

1 pkg. active dry yeast
1 tsp. ground cardamom
1/4 c. butter
1 egg

3 c. all-purpose flour, divided
1 c. milk, divided
1/2 tsp. salt
2/3 c. sugar, divided

In a large bowl, combine 3/4 cup all-purpose flour, 1 package active dry yeast and 1 teaspoon ground cardamom. Stirring constantly, heat 3/4 cup milk, 1/4 cup butter, 1/3 cup sugar and 1/2 teaspoon salt until just warm. Add to flour mixture. Add 1 slightly beaten egg. Beat at low speed of electric mixer for 30 seconds. Beat 3 minutes at high speed. With a spoon, stir in as much of 2 to 2 1/4 cups all-purpose flour as you can. Turn onto a floured surface; knead in enough remaining flour to make moderately soft dough that is smooth and elastic, about 5 minutes. Shape into a ball and place in a greased bowl, turning once to grease top. Cover; let rise till double, about 1 1/4 hours.

Punch dough down, divide into six pieces. Cover; let rest 10 minutes. Shape each piece into a rope about 8" long. Place three ropes on a greased baking sheet and braid loosely so the dough has room to expand.

Pinch ends firmly and tuck under so the braids won't come apart while baking.   Repeat with the remaining three ropes on another greased baking sheet. Cover and let rise until nearly doubled; about 40 minutes.

Lightly brush with remaining milk and sprinkle with 1 tablespoon sugar. Bake in a 375° oven about 20 minutes or golden brown. Cool on a wire rack.

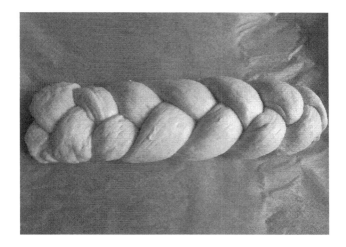

BREADS & ROLLS

JOAN'S ROLLS   Joan Silver

These are my famous rolls!

2 Tbsp. yeast	2 Tbsp. sugar
1/2 c. warm water	1/2 c. Crisco®
1/2 c. sugar	2 eggs
1 c. hot water	2 tsp. salt
4 1/2 c. flour	

Dissolve yeast, sugar and warm water. Set aside.

Cream together sugar, Crisco® and eggs. Add hot water. Mix well, and then add yeast mixture. Add in the salt. Fold in the flour

Knead well and set aside for 1 hour or until double in size. Punch down and roll out and cut.

Bake at 375˚ for 10 to 15 minutes until golden brown.

BREADS & ROLLS

MORMON MUFFINS
Wendy Swanson

My mother gave me this recipe, and I usually cut it in two, or even fourths, because it makes so much! These muffins are delicious with honey butter. Try them for breakfast with a piece of fruit, or even better, have one for lunch with a nice green salad.

2 c. boiling water	1 c. butter
5 c. flour	4 c. All-Bran cereal
2 c. 40% Bran Flakes cereal	1 c. chopped nuts
5 tsp. baking soda	4 eggs
1 qt. buttermilk	2 c. sugar
1 tsp. salt	1 c. chopped dates (optional)

Add soda to the boiling water, then let cool. In a large bowl, cream butter and sugar and add eggs one at a time, mixing well after each addition. Combine flour and salt in a separate bowl. Alternately add flour and buttermilk to the creamed sugar and eggs; mixing well each time. In another large bowl, combine bran and nuts. Then add the cooled water to the bran mixture. Fold the bran mixture into the batter.

Bake in a 375° oven for 15 to 20 minutes.

BREADS & ROLLS

PAULA'S PINEAPPLE–ZUCCHINI BREAD   Wendy Swanson

A good friend of mine, Paula Hansen, used to make this bread for me, and when she moved away, she shared her recipe with me. Paula is no longer with us, but I always think of her whenever I use this recipe.

3 eggs
1 c. oil
2 c. sugar
2 tsp. vanilla
2 c. coarsely shredded, unpeeled
   zucchini
1 1/2 tsp. cinnamon
3/4 tsp. nutmeg

3 c. flour
2 tsp. soda
1 tsp. salt
1/2 tsp. baking powder
1 can (8 1/4 oz.) well-drained
   crushed pineapple
1 c. finely chopped walnuts
1 c. strawberry-infused dried
   cranberries

1/4 c. cinnamon sugar blend (1/4 c. white sugar + 1 Tbsp. cinnamon thoroughly whisked together)

In a large bowl, beat eggs until frothy; add oil, sugar and vanilla; continue beating until mixture is thick and foamy. Stir in zucchini and pineapple. In a separate bowl, stir together flour, soda, salt, baking powder, cinnamon nutmeg, walnuts and cranberries until thoroughly blended. Stir gently into zucchini mixture just until blended.

Spoon batter equally into 2 greased and flour dusted 9x5" loaf pans. Sprinkle cinnamon sugar blend over each loaf.

Bake in a 350° oven for 1 hour or until breads begin to pull away from sides of pans and a wooden skewer inserted in centers comes out clean. completely.

Note: If you can't locate strawberry-infused dried cranberries, any type of dried cranberries will work well.

BREADS & ROLLS

OATMEAL MUFFINS   Tamara Rogers

1 c. flour	1/4 c. sugar
3 tsp. baking powder	1/2 tsp. salt
1 c. quick cooking rolled oats	1 slightly beaten egg
1 c. milk	3 Tbsp. salad oil

Sift or mix: Flour with sugar, baking powder and salt.

Add quick cooking rolled oats. Add slightly beaten egg, milk and salad oil; stirring just to moisten.

Fill 12 greased muffin holders 2/3 full.

Bake at 425° for about 15 minutes.

BREADS & ROLLS

SCHOOL LUNCH ROLLS   Marlene Mason Wood
From East Elementary School lunch in St. George, Utah

Flour	20 lbs.	25 lbs.	30 lbs.	50 lbs.
Sugar	2 c.	2 1/4 c.	2 1/2 c.	3 c.
Yeast	3/4 c.	1 c.	1 c.	1 1/2 c.
Water	2 gal.	2 gal.	2 1/2 gal.	4 gal.
Dry milk	1 1/2 lbs.	2 lbs.	2 lbs.	3 lbs.
Eggs	20	22	24	44
Shortening	1 1/2 lbs.	2 lbs.	2 lbs.	3 lbs.
Salt	3/4 c.	1 c.	1 c.	2 c.

I worked at school lunch for 27 years. This is one of our recipes. 40 lbs. of flour makes enough rolls for 450 children.

Now count your blessings that you only have to cook for as many as you do!

BREADS & ROLLS

SOUR CREAM BANANA NUT BREAD   Gail Smith

2 c. flour
1 1/3 c. sugar
3/4 tsp. salt
1 tsp. baking powder
1 tsp. baking soda
2 eggs

1/4 c. butter
1 c. sour cream
1 tsp. vanilla
1 c. mashed banana (2)
1/2 c. nuts

Cream butter and sugar, then add eggs and vanilla. Beat. Alternate dry ingredients and sour cream. Beat well after each addition. Add bananas and nuts. Put in greased pans.

Bake in a 350° oven for 30-40 minutes (depending on the size pans you use).

Let cool then frost with CREAM CHEESE FROSTING recipe on the next page.

BREADS & ROLLS

CREAM CHEESE FROSTING   Gail Smith

3 Tbsp. butter, softened
1 – 3 oz. pkg. cream cheese, softened
1 2/3 c. powdered sugar, sifted
1/2 tsp. vanilla

Beat softened butter and cream cheese until well blended.

Add powdered sugar and vanilla. Beat until creamy.

BREADS & ROLLS

SOUR DOUGH BREAD   Wendy Swanson

This recipe takes some planning as the starter needs to ferment for 2 days.

2 c. flour
3 Tbsp. sugar
1 tsp. salt

Mix above ingredients together. Add enough water to make a thin batter.
Set in a warm place to ferment. This will take about 48 hours.

1 tsp. soda
flour

Stir in soda and add enough flour to make a stiff dough. Knead and
shape into small loaves.

Place each loaf into a greased, small loaf pan. Set in a warm place until
double in size.
Bake in a 350° oven for 20 to 25 minutes.

*Don't worry about the soured smell of the fermented liquid, the soda and
baking does away with it.*

MAIN DISHES

MAIN DISHES

BAKED PORK CHOPS with APPLES and STUFFING

Wendy Swanson

4 pork chops
1 tsp. mustard
2 tart apples
2 c. soft bread crumbs
2 Tbsp. chopped onion
1/8 tsp. sage
1/2 tsp. salt

Trim fat from pork chops. Place in a greased casserole dish. Spread with mustard. Cover with thin apple slices.

Make a stuffing of bread crumbs, onion, sage and salt; with enough water to moisten. Put stuffing on top of apples.

Cover and bake in a 350° oven for 30 minutes. Uncover and continue to bake for 15 minutes to brown.

MAIN DISHES

BAKED POTATO CASSEROLE   Marlene Mason Wood

My Aunt Deon Taylor's recipe. She was a wonderful cook, and like a grandma to me.

6 slices of bacon, cooked crispy and crumbled
2 c. grated cheddar cheese
2 c. dairy sour cream
1 stick butter, softened
2 Tbsp. green onion
1/2 tsp. salt

Combine above ingredients thoroughly. Serve with baked potatoes.

MAIN DISHES

BEEF STROGANOFF   Ruth Snarr

I like this recipe because it's quick and easy to fix in a hurry. Especially when you have to take in a meal to somebody.

1 lb. hamburger
1 can cream of chicken soup (10 1/2 oz.)
1 can cream of mushroom soup (10 1/2 oz.)
1 1/2 c. sour cream

Brown hamburger and season to taste.

Mix all ingredients into a Crock Pot.

Cook on low for a couple of hours.

Serve over rice or noodles.

Sometimes I add the noodles to the mixture.

MAIN DISHES

CABBAGE ROLLS   Judy Call

12 cabbage leaves
1 egg, beaten
1/4 c. minced onion
1 1/4 tsp. salt
1 (8 oz.) can tomato sauce
1 Tbsp. lemon juice

1 c. cooked white rice
1/4 c. milk
1 lb. extra-lean ground beef
1 1/4 tsp. ground black pepper
1 Tbsp. brown sugar
1 tsp. Worcestershire sauce

Bring a large pot of water to a boil. Boil cabbage leaves two minutes; drain. In a large bowl, combine cooked rice, egg, milk, onion, ground beef, salt and pepper. Place about 1/4 cup of meat mixture in center of each cabbage leaf, and roll up, tucking in the ends. *You may need to use a few toothpicks to secure.* Place rolls in a slow cooker.

In a small bowl, mix together tomato sauce, brown sugar, lemon juice and Worcestershire sauce. Pour over cabbage rolls.

Cover and cook on low for 8 to 9 hours.

MAIN DISHES

CHICKEN EDDIE   Gail Ann Jacobsen

1/2 of a 2 pound block of Velveeta®

1 can Rotell tomatoes

1 can cream of chicken soup

1 can chicken broth

1 box of angle hair spaghetti cooked (or your favorite pasta)

1 green pepper and onion chopped and sautéed

Garlic to taste

2 full chicken breasts cooked …. chopped or shredded

Mix the cheese, tomatoes, soup and broth in a pan on low heat until cheese is melted.

Put the cooked pasta in a 13x9 pan that you have sprayed with Pam® first, then the chicken and sautéed veggies. Pour the melted cheese, soup and broth over all. Top with French's crunchy onions.

Warm in a 400º oven until warmed thru….looking bubbly and slightly browned.

MAIN DISHES

CHICKEN ENCHILADAS   Wendy Swanson

2 c. cooked and shredded chicken breast
1 pkg. cream cheese
1 c. salsa
6 corn or flour tortillas
1 c. shredded Monterey Jack cheese
1 c. shredded Colby Jack cheese
1 can enchilada sauce

In a saucepan combine the cream cheese and salsa. Cook and stir over medium heat until well blended. Stir in the shredded chicken breast. Fill tortillas with the mixture and place seam side down in a lightly greased 9x13 baking dish. Pour your favorite enchilada sauce over the top and then spread the cheese on top of that. Cover with aluminum foil and bake in a 350° oven for 30 minutes.

Garnish with sour cream, tomatoes and lettuce if you like, and serve with beans and rice.

MAIN DISHES

CHICKEN with STUFFING CASSEROLE   Joan Silver

2 c. cooked chicken cut into bite-sized
pieces
1 can evaporated milk
1 c. slivered, toasted almonds
(for the top)

2 cans of cream of chicken soup
1 c. sour cream
4 tsp. dried onions
2 tsp. lemon juice

Mix these ingredients together, while saving some of the toasted almonds and put in a 13 x 9 glass casserole dish.

Stove Top stuffing ~ 1 chicken and 1 cornbread
1 c. chopped celery
1/2 c. chopped onion

Cook celery and onion in 1/4 c. butter until transparent. Prepare the stuffing according to the directions on the box.

Mix together and place on top of the other ingredients. Top with the remaining toasted almonds.

Bake at 350° for 30 minutes or more until heated through.

MAIN DISHES

COCONUT SHRIMP CURRY   Wendy Swanson

2 Tbsp. olive oil
1 c. chopped onion
2 Tbsp. minced garlic
1/2 tsp. each: paprika, garam masala, cumin seeds and ground turmeric
1 lb. medium shrimp, peeled and deveined
1 can (13.5 oz.) coconut milk
1 tsp. salt
3 c. cooked basmati rice
1/4 c. cilantro leaves

Heat oil in a large saucepan over medium heat. Cook onion until softened. Add garlic, spices and shrimp. Cook; stirring until fragrant, about 2 minutes.   Add coconut milk and salt; simmer 10 minutes.

Spoon curry mixture over rice. Garnish with cilantro leaves.

MAIN DISHES

CROCK POT CHICKEN

Pat Magleby

1/4 to 1/2 c. butter
3 to 4 chicken breasts
1 pkg. dry zesty Italian dressing mix
1 can cream of mushroom soup
8 oz. cream cheese

Melt butter in cooker. Add chicken breasts and sprinkle with dry zesty Italian dressing mix.

Cook on low for 4 to 5 hours.

Combine and mix well: cream of mushroom soup and cream cheese.

Add to chicken and cook 1 additional hour.

Serve over rice or noodles, or even mashed potatoes.

MAIN DISHES

CROCK POT ROAST BEEF   Gail Ann Jacobsen

This is another favorite dish for my family and it has been passed around to my immediate family and extended family. Enjoy.

3-4 lb. boneless rump roast
1 can cream of mushroom soup
1 can beef gravy
2 Tbsp. vinegar
1 Tbsp. Worcestershire sauce
1/4 c. brown sugar
1/8 tsp. salt
1/8 tsp. pepper
Garlic to taste

Put all ingredients in crock pot and cook at low temperature for 12-14 hours or on high for 8-10 hours.

Thicken the liquid to make gravy.

MAIN DISHES

EASY BAKED ORANGE ROUGHY   Gail Ann Jacobsen

1 1/4 lbs. Orange Roughy Fillets
1 tsp. seasoning salt (or to taste)
Pepper (to taste)
Paprika (to taste)
3 Tbsp. butter, melted

Put fish fillets in a greased 11x7 inch baking dish. Sprinkle with seasoned salt, pepper and paprika. Drizzle with melted butter.

Cover and bake at 400º for 15 to 20 minutes or until fish flakes easily.

MAIN DISHES

ELDORADO CASSEROLE   Gail Ann Jacobsen

1/2 lb. ground beef or turkey
  (I like turkey best--milder taste)
1 c. water
1/2 pkg. taco seasoning

1 pkg. (9-oz.) tortilla chips, crumbled
1 cup shredded cheese

1 medium onion chopped
2 cans (8-oz.) tomato sauce
1/4 tsp. chili powder
1 can corn, drained
  (Mexican style corn is good)
1 cup sour cream

Preheat oven to 375°. Spray a baking dish (I used an 8" sq. dish) with nonstick cooking spray. Brown the beef and onion, drain grease. Add tomato sauce, water, chili powder and taco seasoning, mix well. Simmer for 2-3 min or until thickened. Spread 1/3 of the beef mixture in the baking dish, 1/3 of the corn, chips, sour cream and cheese. Repeat the layers ending with cheese.

Bake for 25-30 minutes or until bubbly and the top is golden.

MAIN DISHES

FRESH VEGETABLE CASSEROLE   Joan Silver

This is so good!

3 c. broccoli flowerets – cooked and drained
2 c. sliced carrots – cooked tender crisp and drained
1/2 lb. button mushrooms – parboiled 2-3 minutes, drained
2 c. small white onions – parboiled 2-3 minutes, drained

In a 2 quart shallow baking dish, toss well; all the vegetables.

3 Tbsp. cornstarch	1/4 c. corn oil margarine
1/2 tsp. salt	2 Tbsp. lemon juice
1/8 tsp. pepper	2 Tbsp. chopped parsley
2 c. milk	

In a 2 quart saucepan stir together cornstarch, salt and pepper. Gradually add milk until smooth. Add margarine, stirring constantly. Boil 1 minute. Stir in lemon juice and parsley. Spoon over vegetables. Sprinkle with crumb dressing. Bake at 350° for 25-30 minutes or until vegetables are tender.

Crumb Topping:

3/4 c. soft bread crumbs	3 Tbsp. chopped parsley
1/3 c. grated Parmesan cheese	2 Tbsp. melted margarine

MARINATED CHICKEN (or TURKEY) BREAST TENDERS

Gail Ann Jacobsen

1 pkg. chicken or turkey breast tenders (98% fat free, boneless, skinless)
1 c. Sprite® (I use diet or Zero)
1/2 c. oil
1/4 c. soy sauce (I use lite)

Combine Sprite, oil and soy sauce. Pour over chicken or turkey. Cover and refrigerate at least 8 hours or overnight. Turn meat occasionally in marinade to insure equal flavoring throughout.

Barbecue over hot coals, broil in oven or pan fry on both sides until meat is white inside.

DO NOT OVERCOOK!

MAIN DISHES

ENCHILADA CAKE   Gail Ann Jacobsen

1 lb. extra lean ground beef
1 lb. ground turkey
2 medium potatoes, cooked and shredded
Salt, pepper, garlic salt, oregano, paprika and Chile
    powder to taste
3 cans enchilada sauce (in shallow pan to keep hot)
2 pkgs. corn tortillas
1 can chopped black olives
Cheese (your choice) for grating (I use a lot because we like cheese.)

Brown the beef and turkey. Mix in the shredded potatoes and spices. Pour the 3 cans of enchilada sauce into a shallow pan and heat.

Dip 6 tortillas in the hot enchilada sauce and lay them in a 9x13 greased baking pan/dish. Layer a portion of the meat mixture, olives and grated cheese. Repeat three times.

Bake in a 350° preheated oven for about 30 minutes or the cheese is bubbly. While the cake is baking, prepare the sauce.

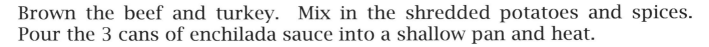

SAUCE TO SERVE WITH THE BAKED ENCHILADA CAKE:

2 cans taco sauce   1 can tomato sauce
1 can chopped green chilies

Combine the taco sauce, tomato sauce and green chilies in a saucepan. Heat and stir occasionally, but do not boil.

Slice the Enchilada cake and serve with the sauce; along with shredded lettuce, chopped onions, chopped tomatoes, sour cream and guacamole if desired. This will serve at least 12 or more depending on the portion size.

My ex-husband went to the Buster Welch Cutting Horse school in Throckmorton, TX in November of 1968, along with myself, a three-year-old daughter and a four-month-old daughter. It was a very good experience. We traveled from Simla, CO to Throckmorton, TX in a pickup with a camper shell on it. It was also our sleeping arrangement. When we arrived there, we ate, etc. with the other people there in a very nice large home. Fortunately, we did not take a horse; however, the horse probably would have been easier to care for as compared to two young children. We were there for a week and I'm sure that my husband learned a great deal. I liked watching the man that was teaching and the men that were learning. At one of the meals, we had this Enchilada Cake. Our family has really liked it, so we have it a lot.

MAIN DISHES

GUAM CHICKEN   Joan Silver

I lived on Guam for two years; this was a favorite dish!

1 c. soy sauce

1 c. water

1 c. vinegar

1/2 onion, diced

1/2 tsp. salt

1/2 tsp. pepper

1/2 tsp. minced garlic

Combine ingredients together and pour over skinned chicken pieces. Marinade overnight (or quick method; heat mixture and soak skinned chicken for 3 – 4 hours).

Build a medium-hot fire in a charcoal grill or heat a gas grill to medium-high. Cook chicken, turning, until browned, about 8 minutes.

MAIN DISHES

MAMA JOANIE'S ITALIAN SPAGHETTI and MEAT BALLS

Joan Silver

Meat Balls:

1/2 lb. hamburger

1 slightly beaten egg

1/4 c. warm water

1/2 tsp. basil

½ c. fine dry bread crumbs

1/4 c. Parmesan cheese, grated

1 1/2 tsp. salt

1/4 tsp. pepper

Combine the above ingredients and form into 1 inch balls. Brown and simmer until sauce is together.

Sauce:

3 1/2 c. tomato juice

1/4 c. onions, chopped

2 tsp. chopped parsley

1/4 tsp. anise seed

1 (6 oz.) can tomato paste

2 cloves minced garlic

1 tsp. oregano

Simmer together at least 1/2 hour. Serve with Parmesan cheese.

MAIN DISHES

POTLUCK RIBS   Anna Frezza

Barbara Fossum, my dearest and closest friend for many years, passed away not long ago. By the time we met, we had both lost our husbands and were alone. We soon found that we also had many interests in common...travel, religion, game nights and cooking. We joined several groups that got together regularly to pursue those interests. One group held a monthly game of Hand and Foot that involved a lot of fun play and a potluck lunch. Barbara always prepared these ribs for this group and many others over the years. The ribs were always the favorite dish on the potluck table. I now make them for both my family when they visit and for potlucks that I attend today. Barbara is missed very much but she makes me happy each time I eat these tasty, tender ribs.

3-4 lbs. pork spareribs
1 c. maple syrup
1/3 c. soy sauce
3 Tbsp. sweet cooking wine
  (Kikkoman Aji-Mirrin in Asian food aisle)
1 Tbsp. garlic powder
2 tsp. salt
1/2 tsp. sugar

Bring ribs, and enough water to completely cover them, to a boil in a large Dutch oven, covered. Reduce heat and simmer 30 minutes.

Remove ribs and place in a lightly greased 13'x9' pan.

Stir together remaining six ingredients and pour over ribs.

Bake uncovered at 325° for 1 hour.

Note: Sauce is fairly thin. If you prefer a thicker sauce, you can stir in a little diluted cornstarch until at desired consistency.

MAIN DISHES

PINWHEELS

Wendy Swanson

When I think of "comfort food" this is what I think of. This was a favorite in my family; my brothers would have liked to have it every night.

1 lb. hamburger
1 pkg. brown gravy mix
2 1/4 c. Original Bisquick™ mix

1 can mixed vegetables
2/3 c. milk

Brown the hamburger.

BISCUIT MIX:
Stir the Bisquick and milk together until a soft dough forms. Turn out on a surface dusted with Bisquick. Knead 10 times. Roll dough to a 1/2" thickness. Evenly spread hamburger and drained vegetables onto dough. Roll up like a jelly roll and make 12 slices.

Bake in a 425° preheated oven for 20 to 25 minutes. Just before they are done cooking prepare the brown gravy mix according to package directions. Serve hot with the gravy.

MAIN DISHES

QUICK CHILI   Gail Ann Jacobsen

This is our very favorite Chili, and the easiest there ever was to prepare.

1 pkg. of your favorite chili seasoning
1 lb. hamburger (I use half ground beef and half ground turkey.)
1 onion, chopped
2 cans meatless chili sauce
2 cans Campbell's® tomato soup
1 can diced tomatoes

Brown the meat and onions. Mix with all the remaining ingredients.
Simmer for 1 hour.

MAIN DISHES

SPAGHETTI SQUASH CHOW MEIN   Gail Ann Jacobsen

Ingredients:

6 c. cooked spaghetti squash

3 cloves garlic, minced

2 tsp. freshly grated ginger

2 Tbsp. olive oil

3 stalks celery, sliced diagonally

1 c. shredded carrots

1/4 c. low sodium soy sauce

1 pkt. Splenda® or Stevia

1/4 tsp. white pepper

1/3 onion, diced

2 c. shredded cabbage

Cut spaghetti squash in half lengthwise and scoop out seeds. Lay skin side up in a 13x9" Pyrex pan and pour 1/2 inch of water in the bottom.

Bake at 400º for 30-40 minutes, until flesh is very tender. Let cool a little bit so that it is easier to handle.

> (You can also cook the spaghetti squash in the microwave. Punch holes in the squash and microwave for 6 minutes on one side and 6 minutes on the other side.)

Once done, scoop out flesh with a fork so it breaks apart into strings, set aside.

In a small bowl, whisk together soy sauce, garlic, sweetener, ginger and white pepper. Set aside.

Heat olive oil in a large skillet over medium high heat. Add onion, celery and carrots, cook stirring often until tender, about 3-4 minutes. Stir in cabbage until heated through, about 1 minute.

Add in spaghetti squash and soy sauce mixture until well combined, about 2 minutes. Serve immediately.

Makes 6 servings

I cooked Shrimp to have as our meat with this. Was very good. There was enough that we were able to have it for 2 meals.

MAIN DISHES

SLOPPY JOES
Judy Call

1 lb. ground beef
1 medium onion, chopped
1 1/2 Tbsp. flour
1 c. Coca-Cola® (that's right)
  or Pepsi® or Dr. Pepper® (optional)

2/3 c. catsup
2 Tbsp. vinegar
1 Tbsp. Worcestershire sauce
2 level tsp. dry mustard

In a skillet brown the meat and onions. Drain the excess fat. Add the remaining ingredients and stir to mix. Cover and simmer for 30 minutes.

Serve hot in hamburger buns. Drink the rest of the Coca-Cola® over ice.

They'll come back for more!

MAIN DISHES

SUNDRIED TOMATO PESTO OVER SQUASH PASTA

Wendy Swanson

1 c. sundried tomatoes, soaked in water for 2 hours
1 c. fresh basil
1/2 c. pine nuts
1 tsp. chopped garlic
1 tsp. sea salt
4 Tbsp. fresh squeezed lemon juice
1/3 c. extra virgin olive oil

In a food processor, combine all ingredients (except the extra virgin olive oil). Pulse until blended together. Drizzle in olive oil and pulse again.

Serve this raw recipe over traditional pasta, or use a spiralizer to make noodles out of a summer squash or zucchini.

This raw recipe is full of flavor and comes together quickly.

MAIN DISHES

SWEET & SOUR GRILLED SHRIMP & VEGGIES   Wendy Swanson

2 lbs. fresh or frozen large shrimp in the shell
*Assorted fresh vegetables, cut into bite-sized pieces
10 oz. currant jelly
1 Tbsp. soy sauce
3 Tbsp. vinegar
1/2 tsp. ground ginger
1/2 tsp. garlic powder

Thaw shrimp if frozen. Peel and devein shrimp. In a saucepan, combine jelly, soy sauce, vinegar, ginger, and garlic powder. Heat and stir until boiling. While mixture is cooling, thread shrimp and veggies on skewers. Brush the sweet & sour mixture over the shrimp and veggies and grill for 4 or 5 minutes. Turn shrimp and veggies over and brush with the sweet & sour mixture. Grill 4 to 5 minutes more.

Serve with white or jasmine rice if desired.

* I like to use bell peppers, onions, carrots, zucchini & sometimes pineapple.

MAIN DISHES

VEGETABLE CHOW MEIN   Wendy Swanson

This recipe was my great grandmother, Laura Martina Grieve Musgrave's, with one slight change. She always added pieces of cooked chicken breast; as did my grandmother and mother.

1 small red onion, chopped	1 - 2 Tbsp. oil
2 c. chopped celery	2 c. bean sprouts
1 - 2 bell peppers, chopped	1/4 c. soy sauce
1 can water chestnuts	2 Tbsp. brown sugar
2 Tbsp. cornstarch	1/3 c. water

Crispy Chow Mein noodles (I like China Boy brand)

Heat oil in a large skillet. Sauté the onion in the oil. While the onion is sautéing, whisk together the cornstarch, brown sugar, soy sauce and water. Add the celery and pepper to the onion. Pour in the soy sauce mixture. Bring to a simmer, stirring frequently. After about 5 to 7 minutes, add the water chestnuts and bean sprouts. Make sure all the vegetables are well-coated with the sauce. If the sauce is getting too thick, add a little more water. Let simmer for 3 to 4 minutes. Remove from heat and spoon vegetables and sauce over Chow Mein noodles.

MAIN DISHES

VEGETARIAN TACO CASSEROLE   Wendy Swanson

1 can pinto beans
1 can black beans, drained and rinsed
1 c. salsa
1/2 c. sour cream
2 tsp. chili powder
1 small can chopped green chilies
3 c. broken tortilla chips
1 c. cheddar cheese, grated
1 c. Monterey jack cheese, grated
Shredded lettuce
Tomato

Mix beans, salsa, sour cream, chili powder and green chilies. In a casserole dish; layer half the bean mixture, half the chips, and half of each cheese. Repeat the layers.

Bake in a 350° oven for 25 minutes. Serve topped with lettuce and tomato.

DESSERTS

DESSERTS

APPLE HILL CAKE   Anna Frezza

In the hills of Northern California, above nearby Placerville, lies a community of over 50 family farms that united years ago to form the Apple Hill Growers. Each year from August through December, they invite visitors to come and enjoy their apple harvest, bake shops, freshly pressed apple cider, craft fair and much more. This cake, by itself, was worth the short trip I made with friends to spend a day at Apple Hill for each of the ten years that I lived in Placer County.

2 c. sugar (I reduce to 1 1/2 cups of half white and half brown sugar)
1/2 c. vegetable oil
2 eggs
4 c. diced crisp apples
2 c. flour
2 tsp. baking soda
1 tsp. nutmeg
2 tsp. cinnamon
1 tsp. salt
1 1/2 c. chopped walnuts

Preheat oven to 350°. Grease a 9'x13' pan. Combine sugar, oil and eggs in a large bowl, stirring until well mixed. Add diced apples and nuts to this mixture. Sift together flour, baking soda, nutmeg, cinnamon and salt, then add to bowl. Stir to form a batter - do not overmix. Pour into pan. Bake one hour, or until golden and cake is set.

Let cool before serving.

Delicious warm as is, with whipped cream; or my favorite, spread with cream cheese frosting.

DESSERTS

APPLE DUMPLINGS   Joan Silver

This is my husband, Gerald Silver's recipe. It is his to make and we all love it!

Pare, core and slice 6 Granny Smith apples.

Make syrup of:

2 c. water	1/4 tsp. cinnamon
2 c. sugar	1/4 tsp. nutmeg
1/4 c. butter	

and boil for 3 minutes.

Pastry:

2 c. flour	3/4 c. shortening
2 tsp. baking powder	1/2 c. milk
1 tsp. salt	

Mix and roll 1/4 inch thick. Cut into 5" squares. Arrange apple slices on each square. Sprinkle with cinnamon, sugar and nutmeg; dot with butter. Fold corners to center and pinch with wet fingers. Place in greased baking dish. Pour syrup over dumplings and bake in a moderate oven (375°) for 40 to 45 minutes.

DESSERTS

CHERRY DUMP CAKE   Gail Ann Jacobsen

1 can (20 oz.) crushed pineapple
1 can (21 oz.) cherry pie filling
1 box yellow cake mix
1 stick plus 2 Tbsp. butter, melted
Chopped nuts...your choice and amount

Grease a 9x13 baking pan. Spread pineapple evenly over the bottom of pan. Pour cherry pie filling over pineapple. Spread dry cake mix over cherries. Drizzle melted butter over cake mix. Sprinkle chopped nuts over top. Bake at 375° for 45-50 min. until golden brown.

Makes 12 servings.

DESSERTS

CHERRY ENCHILADAS
Wendy Swanson

6 flour tortillas
1/2 c. butter
1/2 c. brown sugar

1 can (21 oz.) cherry pie filling
1/2 c. sugar
1/2 c. water

Spread pie filling down the center of tortillas. Fold both ends over filling and then roll up to form enchiladas. Place seam side down in a lightly greased 8' x 8' pan.

In a saucepan, melt butter, then add the sugar, brown sugar and water. Stir constantly bringing liquid to a boil. Reduce to low heat and simmer 2 – 3 minutes. Pour sauce over enchiladas.

Allow the sauce to cool to room temperature and preheat oven to 350°. Bake for 15 – 20 minutes or until golden brown.

Serve warm with a scoop of vanilla ice cream or whipped cream.

DESSERTS

EASY RASPBERRY PIE   Wendy Swanson

This recipe comes from my great grandmother, Laura Martina Grieve Musgrave. She didn't have a lot of spare time to prepare desserts for her family. My great grandfather died in 1942, leaving her with three young children to raise, so she went to work at the Defense Depot in Ogden, Utah. She retired after working there for 20 years.

1 Tbsp. gelatin
1/2 c. sugar
1 1/2 c. fresh raspberries
1 c. whipping cream

1 1/2 Tbsp. lemon juice
3 Tbsp. cold water
Dash of salt
Graham cracker crust

Soften gelatin in cold water; then dissolve over hot water. Add sugar, raspberries, lemon juice and salt.

Chill until partly set, then add 1/2 cup of whipped cream.

Pour into graham cracker crust. Chill until firm. Serve with remaining whipped cream on top.

DESSERTS

FROZEN STRAWBERRY SQUARES   Gail Smith

1 c. flour   1/4 c. brown sugar, packed
1/2 c. pecans or walnuts   1/2 c. margarine or butter
  (coarsely chopped)

Combine flour and brown sugar. Cut in butter until it forms crumbs. Stir in nuts. Spread in a shallow pan (9x13) and bake at 350° for 15 minutes. Stir often so it doesn't burn. Remove from oven and cool, crush crumbs and set aside.

In a large bowl, combine:
2 egg whites   1 scant cup sugar
1 - 10 oz. pkg. (partially defrosted) strawberries

Beat until stiff and thick (over 5 minutes). It will look like a big, pink, fluffy cloud.

Stir in:

1 Tbsp. lemon juice
1 c. heavy cream, whipped or Cool Whip
(cream can be left out of the dessert)

Spread 1/2 of the crumbs in pan.

Add filling. Sprinkle the rest of crumbs on top.

Cover and freeze for several hours.

Serve with whipping cream or Cool Whip on top.

DESSERTS

FUDGE NUT BARS

Gail Ann Jacobsen

I got this recipe from my Mother-in-law when I was first married after she had made them. They are so, so good. . . . .and has been a favorite of our family since then.

1 12 oz. pkg. semi-sweet chocolate chips

3 Tbsp. butter

2 c. packed brown sugar

1 c. butter

1 tsp. salt

3 to 4 c. regular oatmeal

1 14 oz. can Eagle Brand milk

3 /4 c. chopped nuts

2 tsp. vanilla

2 eggs

2 1/2 c. flour

1 tsp. baking powder

Melt together over lowest heat, chocolate chips, Eagle Brand milk and the 3 tablespoons butter. When melted remove from heat and stir in vanilla and nuts. Set aside.

Cream together one cup butter, brown sugar and eggs, then stir in flour, baking powder and salt. Add oatmeal a little at a time, mixing well (saving about ¼ of this batter). Put into a 13 x 9 pan that has been greased or sprayed with Pam®.

Spread chocolate mixture over top and dot with saved oatmeal mixture.

Bake at 350° for 25 minutes. When cooled, cut into squares.

ICE CREAM DESSERT   Ruth Snarr

1/2 gallon of ice cream
1 small can of fruit juice (I've used orange, mango, strawberry, raspberry and others juices)

Let ice cream sit until soft.

Let juice melt completely

Mix the two together and pour into a cake pan (I use glass).

Refreeze and serve with a cookie, cake or whatever.

DESSERTS

LION HOUSE CARROT CAKE   Gail Smith

1 c. sugar

2 eggs, beaten

1 c. flour (we often use at least part whole wheat flour with good results)

1/4 c. each: (often omit one of these)
  Ground coconut
  Pecans or walnuts
  Raisins

1/2 c. oil (or applesauce)

1 1/2 c. grated carrot

1/2 tsp. salt

1 tsp. cinnamon

1 tsp. baking soda

Combine sugar and oil. Add eggs, mix well. Add carrots. Slowly stir in sifted dry ingredients. Add ground coconut, nuts and raisins.

Pour batter into a lightly greased and floured 9x9 cake pan (we like to use our bundt pan).

Bake at 400° for 20-30 minutes or until tests done. When cool spread with orange-butter glaze. (Recipe on the following page.)

DESSERTS

ORANGE BUTTER GLAZE   Gail Smith

1 1/2 Tbsp. milk
1 1/4 cups powdered sugar
1/2 tsp. grated orange rind
1 Tbsp. butter

Heat milk and butter together. Stir in sugar and mix until smooth.

Add orange juice and rind. Beat until shiny. Add a drop or two more liquid if need to make desired spreading (or drizzling) consistency.

Makes about 1/2 cup, or enough to glaze top of 10 inch tube cake, or 8-9-inch square cake, or a loaf pan.

DESSERTS

MOM'S HOT WATER GINGERBREAD CAKE   Gail Smith

1/3 c. shortening
1 2/3 c. flour
1 tsp. baking soda
1/2 tsp. salt
1 tsp. ginger
2/3 c. hot water (simmer)

1 tsp. cinnamon
1/2 tsp. cloves
1/3 c. sugar
1 egg
2/3 c. light molasses

Cream shortening; gradually add sugar, mixing until creamy. Beat egg until light. Add to creamed shortening mixture and beat well. Combine molasses and hot water and add dry ingredients alternately with molasses mixture.

Bake in a 350° preheated oven for 35-40 minutes in a greased and floured 8 or 9" pan.

DESSERTS

ORANGE CAKE   Wendy Swanson

A quote to live by: "I'm careful of the words I say, I keep them soft and sweet, I never know from day to day, which ones I'll have to eat."

1/2 c. shortening	1 c. dates
2 c. flour	1 tsp. soda
1 1/2 c. sugar	1 orange and rind
2 eggs, slightly beaten	1/2 tsp. salt
2 tsp. vanilla	1 c. hot water

Grate the orange peel and then juice the orange. Cream together shortening, sugar, salt and vanilla. Add slightly beaten eggs, dates and orange zest. Stir in sifted flour. Last, dissolve the soda in hot water and add to the mixture. Bake in a 9x13 greased pan at 350° for 35 to 40 minutes.

ORANGE ICING

1/2 c. orange juice	1/2 c. confectioners' sugar

Add the juice from the orange to orange juice to make 1/2 cup. Mix with the confectioners' sugar and pour on cake while still hot.

DESSERTS

PEACH COBBLER   Wendy Swanson

I can't think of anything that could taste more wonderful than a fresh, juicy peach cobbler on a warm summer night.

Filling:

1/2 c. brown sugar	1 Tbsp. flour
1 tsp. cinnamon	Dash of nutmeg
1 tsp. grated lemon zest	1/4 tsp. salt
6 c. fresh peach slices	1 Tbsp. fresh lemon juice

Topping:

2 c. flour	1/2 c. sugar
2 tsp. baking powder	3/4 tsp. salt
1 1/2 sticks of cold butter, cut into small pieces	1/2 c. water

Preheat oven to 425°. Spray a 9-inch square or round baking dish with cooking spray.

For the filling, mix the brown sugar, flour, cinnamon, nutmeg, lemon zest and salt in a large bowl. Add the sliced peaches and lemon juice. Gently toss until combined. Pour into the baking dish and bake about 15 minutes or until bubbly.

While the filling is cooking, prepare the topping. Mix the flour, sugar, baking powder and salt in a medium bowl. Cut in the small pieces of butter with a pastry blender until coarse crumbs are formed. Add the water, and stir just until the dry ingredients are moist.

Remove the filling from the oven. Drop the topping by heaping tablespoons onto the peach filling. Sprinkle two tablespoons of sugar over the top of the dough. Bake about 20 minutes, or until the topping is golden brown. Serve warm or at room temperature.

APPLE CRISP   Wendy Swanson

6 to 8 apples	1 tsp. cinnamon
1/2 c. water	1 c. sugar
3/4 c. flour	1/2 c. butter

Peel and core the apples and slice into a buttered casserole dish, adding cinnamon and water. Work together until crumbly the following ingredients: sugar, flour and butter. Spread over the apples and bake uncovered at 375° for one hour and 25 minutes or at 400° for 1 hour.

For a change, try using Asian pears in place of the apples; just reduce the cooking time by 5 minutes.

DESSERTS

PIE CRUST   Joan Silver

I got this recipe from the "Pie Lady" at Cherry Hill in Farmington, Utah.

6 c. flour   3 tsp. salt
3 c. shortening   1 1/2 c. water

Mix flour and salt together; add shortening. Mix until it resembles small peas. Add water. Mix until blended.

Bake at 375° on bottom shelf. Bake shells for 8 – 10 minutes.

This recipe makes 6 shells.

DESSERTS

POPPY SEED CAKE
Joan Silver

1 pkg. yellow cake mix
1 small pkg. instant French vanilla
  pudding
4 eggs
1 c. sour cream

1/2 c. water
1 tsp. rum or almond extract
1/2 c. butter
1/4 c. poppy seeds

Combine all ingredients and beat for 5 minutes on medium speed.

Grease and flour bundt cake pan. Bake at 350° for 45 minutes. Cool 15 minutes. Turn cake over onto a plate.

You can also add a glaze on top by mixing a little butter, milk powdered sugar and vanilla.

DESSERTS

RASPBERRY WALNUT TORTE   Jan Slocum

This is great. It sounds hard, but really isn't. My family loves it.

Tart Base:

1 c. flour

1/2 c. butter

1/3 c. powdered sugar

Raspberry Filling:

1 10 oz. pkg. frozen raspberries,
  thawed (save the liquid)

3/4 c. chopped walnuts

2 eggs

1 c. sugar

1/2 tsp. baking powder

1/2 tsp. salt

1 tsp. vanilla

1/4 c. flour

Raspberry Sauce:

1/2 c. sugar

1/2 c. water

2 Tbsp. corn starch

1 Tbsp. lemon juice

Tart base directions:
Combine flour, powdered sugar, and softened butter; blend well. Press into a 9" ungreased square or round pan. Bake in a 350° preheated oven for 15 minutes. Cool.

Raspberry filling directions:
Drain raspberries and save liquid. Spread berries over crust, sprinkle with walnuts. Combine the remaining filling ingredients at low speed and pour over walnuts. Bake in a 350° preheated oven for 35 to 40 minutes until golden brown. Cool.

Raspberry sauce directions:
Combine sugar, cornstarch, water and the liquid saved from the drained raspberries in a saucepan. Cook until thick and clear. Stir in the lemon juice and cool.

Serve the torte with whipped cream and raspberry sauce.

DESSERTS

ROCKY ROAD FUDGE BARS   Joan Silver

1/2 c. butter or margarine, melted
1 square (1 oz.) unsweetened chocolate,
    melted
1 c. sugar
1 c. all-purpose flour
1/2 to 1 c. chopped nuts
1 tsp. baking powder
1 tsp. vanilla
2 eggs

Mix in saucepan in which butter and chocolate were melted.

Grease and flour 13x9-inch pan.

Spread batter in prepared pan.

1 pkg. (8 oz.) cream cheese, softened,
    (reserve 2 oz. for frosting)
1/2 c. sugar
2 Tbsp. all-purpose flour
1/4 c. butter or margarine, softened
1 egg
1/2 tsp. vanilla

Blend in small mixer bowl until smooth and fluffy.

Spread over chocolate batter.

1/4 c. chopped nuts

6 oz. pkg. (1 cup) semi-sweet chocolate
  pieces

Sprinkle over cream cheese.

Bake at 350º for 25 to 35 minutes until toothpick inserted in center comes out clean.

2 c. miniature marshmallows

Sprinkle over baked bars. Bake 2 minutes longer.

1/4 c. butter or margarine

1 square (1 oz.) unsweetened chocolate

Remaining 2 oz. cream cheese

1/4 c. milk

Melt over low heat in large saucepan.

3 c. (1 lb.) powdered sugar

1 tsp. vanilla

Stir into above mixture until smooth. Immediately pour over marshmallows and swirl together. Store in refrigerator.

Makes about 3 dozen bars.

DESSERTS

RHUBARB CAKE

Gail Ann Jacobsen

4 c. rhubarb, 1/2 " cubes
1/2 c. sugar
1 Tbsp. minute tapioca
1/2 yellow cake mix, prepared

Mix rhubarb, sugar and tapioca. Put in 9x13 pan sprayed with Pam®. Pour prepared cake mix over top.

Bake at 350° for 20 minutes.

DESSERTS

UTAH PIONEER CRANBERRY PIE   Wendy Swanson

This recipe was given to me by a good friend. It is more like a cobbler than a traditional pie. She made it for a potluck we attended; it was so delicious that I went back for seconds. I was too late; it was gone!

2 c. fresh cranberries
2/3 c. sugar
1 c. sugar
2 large eggs, lightly beaten
1 stick unsalted butter, melted

3/4 c. chopped pecans
1 c. flour
1/4 tsp. salt
1 tsp. pure almond extract

Preheat oven to 350 and butter a cake pan or pie pan. Add cranberries to the bottom of this pan. Sprinkle in chopped pecans; sprinkle in 2/3 cup sugar. In a bowl, combine flour, a cup of sugar, melted butter, eggs, almond extract and salt. Stir to combine. Pour batter slowly over the top in large ribbon shapes in order to evenly cover the surface.

Bake for 45 minutes or so. A few minutes prior to removing from the over, sprinkle surface with a tablespoon of sugar for extra crunch. Cut into wedges. Serve with ice cream or freshly whipped cream.

DESSERTS

WALNUT CREAM ROLL
Judy Buckles

My mom made this recipe for a special treat when we were kids. Now my kids love it too for special occasions.

1 c. sifted flour	3 egg yolks
1/2 c. sugar	1/3 c. cold water
1/2 c. brown sugar	1 tsp. vanilla
1 1/2 tsp. baking powder	3 egg whites
1/2 tsp. salt	1/2 tsp. cream of tartar
1/4 c. oil	Cream filling
Glaze	1 c. toasted walnuts

Sift flour with sugars, baking powder and salt in a bowl. Make a well in the center and add oil, egg yolks and vanilla. Beat until smooth. Beat egg whites in a bowl with cream of tartar until very stiff. Fold into flour mixture. Pour batter into jelly roll pan lined with foil. Bake at 375° for 15 minutes.

Remove from pan as soon as you remove it from the oven. Lay on a clean dish towel sprinkled with powdered sugar. Carefully peel of foil and roll jelly roll fashion and let cool.

Cream filling:

Beat 1 cup cream with 1/8 tsp. salt and 1 tsp. vanilla until thickened. Add 1/4 cup brown sugar. Add part of toasted nuts. Unroll cake roll. Spread cream filling on cake roll and roll back up.

Glaze:

Beat 2 Tbsp. soft butter, 1 cup powdered sugar and 2 or 3 tsp. hot water.

Spread glaze over top of rolled cake and add additional chopped nuts.

I have used toasted pecans with this recipe and it works just as well.

DESERTS

WINTERTIME RASPBERRY PIE   Wendy Swanson

This is a nice pie to make when fresh raspberries are not in season. The easiest way to ensure a flaky pie crust is to place the shortening in the freezer a day or two before baking your pie. The shortening doesn't actually freeze, but it's as cold as possible.

Pie Crust:

2 c. flour	1 tsp. salt
1 c. shortening – frozen	4 oz. cold water

Raspberry Filling:

1 can raspberry pie filling	1/2 c. sugar
1 pkg. frozen raspberries, thawed	2 1/2 Tbsp. cornstarch
1/2 lemon's juice	1/2 tsp. vanilla

Raspberry filling directions:
Mix the thawed, frozen raspberries, lemon juice, sugar, cornstarch and vanilla. Let sit while you work on the pie crust.

Pie crust directions:
Mix the flour and salt in a large bowl. Cut in the shortening until the mixture looks like a coarse cornmeal. Gradually stir in water until mixture forms a ball. Divide dough in half and form into balls. Wrap one half in plastic and put in the refrigerator. Roll out the other half on a floured surface, being careful not to overwork it. Gently place the dough in a pie pan and prick all over with a fork. Now, roll out the second ball of dough.

Pour the can of raspberry pie filling into the bottom crust. Now add, the other raspberry mixture, taking care not to overfill the crust. Place the second crust on top. Flute the edges and prick all over with a fork. If you want to you can sprinkle a scant amount of sugar over the top crust. Brush pie crust with ice water just before putting in the oven; it will make it even flakier.

Bake in a 400° oven for 40 minutes. If the edges are getting too brown, cover with foil or a pie crust shield for the last 10 minutes.

Tip: To prevent pie crust from shrinking, wrap the edge of the crust under the pan to anchor it.

COOKIES

COOKIES

ALMOND COOKIES   Wendy Swanson

This recipe comes from my great grandmother, Laura Martina Grieve Musgrave. Her original recipe called for lard and only 1 teaspoon of almond extract.

2 3/4 c. flour	1 c. sugar
1/2 tsp. baking soda	1/2 tsp. salt
1 c. shortening	1 egg
2 Tbsp. milk	1 1/2 tsp. almond extract
48 halved or whole almonds	

Stir together the flour, sugar, baking soda and salt. Cut in the shortening until the mixture looks like cornmeal. In a small bowl, combine the slightly beaten egg, milk and almond extract. Add this to the flour mixture and mix well. Shape the dough into one-inch balls (A melon baller works great for this.) Place each piece of dough two inches apart on an ungreased cookie sheet. Place an almond or almond half on top of each cookie; slightly flatten with the bottom of a glass.

Bake in a 325° oven for 17 minutes or just until the edges are turning golden.

COOKIES

AMISH SUGAR COOKIES
Norma Dooley

1 c. butter or margarine
1 c. granulated sugar
2 eggs
4 1/2 c. flour
1 tsp. soda

1 c. vegetable oil
1 c. powdered sugar
1 tsp. vanilla
1 tsp. cream of tartar
1/2 tsp. salt

Beat butter, oil and sugars. Beat in eggs and vanilla.

Combine dry ingredients. Stir dry ingredients into sugar and oil mixture.

Roll small teaspoons of dough into a ball and put on an ungreased cookie sheet. Flatten ball a little.

Bake at 375° for 8 to 10 minutes. Makes about 5 dozen.

COOKIES

BANANA DROP COOKIES
Judy Buckles

I was given this recipe by my mother-in-law. The whole family loves them, and they are a great alternative for ripe bananas over banana nut bread.

2 c. flour
1 1/2 tsp. baking powder
1/2 tsp. cinnamon
1/4 tsp. baking soda
1/4 tsp. salt
1/4 tsp. cloves

1/2 c. butter
1 c. sugar
2 eggs
1/2 tsp. vanilla
2 mashed bananas

Beat butter and sugar until fluffy. Add eggs and vanilla. Beat well. Combine dry ingredients. Add dry ingredients and bananas alternately until well blended.

Drop by teaspoon on greased cookie sheet. Bake at 375° for 10 to 12 minutes.

When cookies are cool, frost with:
2 c. powdered sugar
1/4 c. mashed banana
2 Tbsp. soft butter
1/2 tsp. vanilla

COOKIES

CHERRY WINKS COOKIES   Wendy Swanson

3/4 c. shortening
1 c. sugar
2 eggs
2 Tbsp. milk
1 tsp. vanilla
2 1/4 c. flour
Corn flake crumbs

1 tsp. baking powder
1/2 tsp. soda
1/2 tsp. salt
1 c. chopped nuts
1 c. chopped dates
1/3 c. maraschino cherries

Cream shortening and sugar together, add eggs, milk and vanilla.

Sift dry ingredients together and add chopped cherries, dates and nuts. Combine with wet ingredients.

Roll a teaspoon of the dough into a ball and roll in corn flake crumbs.

Bake at 375° for 12 to 15 minutes.

COOKIES

EASY LEMON COOKIES   Tamara Rogers

1 (18.25 oz.) pkg. lemon cake mix   2 eggs
1/3 c. vegetable oil   1 tsp. lemon extract
1/3 c. confectioners' sugar for decoration

Preheat oven to 375º.

Pour cake mix into a large bowl. Stir in eggs, oil and lemon extract until well blended. Drop teaspoonfuls of dough into a bowl of confectioners' sugar. Roll them around until they're lightly covered. Once sugared, put them on an ungreased cookie sheet.

Bake for 6 to 10 minutes in the preheated oven. The bottoms will be light brown, and the insides chewy.

COOKIES

GINGER MOLASSES COOKIES   Wendy Swanson

3/4 c. shortening   1 c. sugar
1 egg   4 Tbsp. molasses
2 c. flour   1 tsp. salt
1 tsp. cinnamon   2 tsp. soda
1 tsp. ginger   1/4 tsp. cloves

Cream shortening and sugar together, add egg and molasses.

Sift dry ingredients together. Gradually fold in dry ingredients.

Roll a teaspoon of the dough into a ball and dip into sugar. Place on a greased cookie sheet and slightly flatten.

Bake at 350° for 8 to 10 minutes.

COOKIES

DATE FILLED COOKIES   Wendy Swanson

These were a special treat that my mother, Dixie Burke Warren made at Christmastime. All these years later they're still my favorite cookies; even if I do have to make them myself. C'mon Mom; won't you mail me some?

Cookie:

3/4 c. shortening

1/4 c. butter

1 c. sugar

2 eggs

2 tsp. vanilla

3 c. flour

1 tsp. salt

1 tsp. baking powder

Filling:

2 c. chopped dates

3/4 c. sugar

3/4 c. water

1/2 c. walnuts

Juice of one orange

Cookie Directions:

Cream together sugar, butter and shortening. Stir in each egg thoroughly. Add the vanilla. Stir the dry ingredients together. Gradually fold in dry ingredients. Work with 1/2 the dough keeping the remaining chilled. Roll out dough on a surface lightly dusted with a mixture of 1 c. flour and 1/2 c. sugar. Use a round cookie cutter to cut out the dough.

Filling Directions:
Mix chopped dates, walnuts, sugar and water together in a medium saucepan; bring to boil and reduce heat. Cook and stir until thickened. Remove from heat and add orange juice. Let cool.

Place each cookie cut-out on a cookie sheet. Add 1 – 2 Tbsp. of filling on top of each cookie. Don't overfill.

Roll out the remaining dough and cut out with the cookie cutter. Place each cookie cut-out on top of the filling. Seal the edges all the way around with the tines of a fork. To vent, poke the top of each cookie with the fork tines.

Bake at 375° for about 15 minutes, or until the cookies are browning around the edges.

COOKIES

KIM'S COOKIES   Joan Silver

This is my daughter's recipe.

2 c. shortening	2 tsp. vanilla
1 1/2 c. brown sugar	2 tsp. salt
1 1/2 c. sugar	2 tsp. soda
4 eggs	5 1/2 c. flour
2 Tbsp. hot water	chocolate chips

Cream shortening and sugars together. Add eggs, water and vanilla. Add dry ingredients. Stir in chocolate chips.

Bake for 8 – 10 minutes at 375˚.

COOKIES

MEXICAN WEDDING COOKIES   Wendy Swanson

2 c. butter, softened
1/4 c. sugar
2 tsp. water
1/2 tsp. salt
Powdered sugar

1 tsp. vanilla
2 c. flour
1/2 tsp. baking powder
1 c. chopped pecans

Cream butter and gradually add sugar. Add vanilla and water and blend well. Gradually fold in dry ingredients. Add pecans.

Roll a teaspoon of the dough into a ball. Place on a cookie sheet about 1 inch apart. Bake at 375° for 12 minutes.

Let cool until warm and roll in powdered sugar. Freeze for 2 hours and roll again in powdered sugar.

COOKIES

PINEAPPLE COOKIES   Wendy Swanson

1/2 c. shortening

1 egg

2 c. flour

1/2 tsp. salt

1/2 c. crushed pineapple

(Do not drain pineapple)

1 c. brown sugar

1 1/2 tsp. baking powder

1/2 tsp. soda

1/2 c. nuts

1 tsp. vanilla

Combine all ingredients. Drop by teaspoon on greased cookie sheet.

Bake at 400° for 15 minutes.

COOKIES

RAISIN FILLED COOKIES   Wendy Swanson

Cookie:

1 c. sugar

1/2 c. shortening

1 egg, beaten

1 c. milk

3 1/2 c. flour

3 tsp. baking powder

1 tsp. vanilla

1/2 tsp. salt

Cream together sugar and shortening. Add beaten egg, vanilla and milk. Stir the dry ingredients together. Gradually fold in dry ingredients. Roll out dough thin and cut with a round cookie cutter. Place one teaspoon of filling on each cookie and put another cookie on top and seal edges. Bake at 350° until done.

Filling:

1/2 c. sugar

1 tsp. flour

1 c. ground raisins

1 c. chopped nuts

1/2 c. water

Filling Directions:

Combine all ingredients and cook until thickened.

COOKIES

POOR MAN'S COOKIES   Wendy Swanson
(Fattigmands Bakkelser)

This recipe comes to me from my mother who was taught to make these by her mother, who was taught by her Norwegian mother-in-law, my great grandmother, Maren Karoline Helgensen Bjerke. We just called them "Bakkels." They are a traditional Christmas cookie in Norway along with their counterpart, Rich Man's Cookies, which call for the same ingredients, but are prepared quite differently.

You will need a deep-fryer or heavy pot to make these.

Sift together and set aside:
    5 c. flour
    1 tsp. cardamom

Beat until mixture is thick and lemon-colored:

    10 egg yolks

    2 egg whites

    3/4 c. sugar

    2 tsp. brandy extract

(*I generally use 2 tsp. vanilla extract instead. Originally, the recipe called for 3 Tbsp. of brandy.*)

Add slowly, stirring in:

    1 c. heavy cream

Blend in flour mixture 1/2 cup at a time to make a soft dough. Wrap dough in waxed paper and chill overnight in refrigerator.

Set out a deep-fryer or heavy pot filled with oil or shortening *(Great-grandma's original recipe called for lard)* and heat to 365°F.

Meanwhile, roll out the dough a small portion at a time, to 1/2" thickness on a lightly floured surface. Cut into diamond shapes, 5x2". Make a lengthwise slit in the center of the diamond and pull one tip end through it and tuck back under it.

Deep-fry only as many cookies at a time as will float uncrowded one layer deep in fat. Deep-fry 1 to 2 minutes, or until golden brown, turning once during deep-frying time. Drain over fat for a few seconds before removing to absorbent paper. Sprinkle with Vanilla Confectioners' Sugar (see recipe on the following page).

Store in tightly covered containers. Makes about 6 dozen cookies.

COOKIES

VANILLA CONFECTIONERS' SUGAR   Wendy Swanson
(Vanilie Suker)

This is a flavored sugar you can use for dusting cookies, cakes, waffle and doughnuts.

Set out a 1 to 2 qt. container having a tight-fitting cover. Fill with confectioners' sugar.

Wipe with a clean, damp cloth and dry a vanilla bean, about 9" long.

Cut vanilla bean into quarters lengthwise, cut quarters crosswise into thirds. Poke pieces of vanilla bean down into the sugar at irregular intervals. Cover container tightly to store.

The longer the sugar stands, the richer will be the vanilla flavor. If tightly covered, sugar may be stored for several months. When necessary, add more sugar to jar. Replace vanilla bean when aroma is gone.

Note: Dress up the glass jar with raffia and a tag and give it as a gift to your cookie and cake baking friends.

COOKIES

RED VELVET HEART COOKIES   Wendy Swanson

1 c. butter, softened	1 1/4 c. sugar
l2 Tbsp. unsweetened cocoa powder	1 1/2 tsp. baking powder
1/2 tsp. salt	2 eggs
1 Tbsp. red food coloring	1 tsp. vanilla
2 3/4 c. flour	Powdered sugar

In a large mixing bowl, beat butter for 30 seconds. Add sugar, cocoa, baking powder and salt. Beat until combined.

Beat in eggs, food coloring and vanilla until combined. Beat in as much flour as you can with the mixer. Stir in any remaining flour. Divide dough in half and cover. Chill dough for 1 hour.

On a floured surface, roll half the dough at a time to 1/4" thickness. Cut out dough using a 2 1/2 to 4" heart-shaped cookie cutter. Place cutouts 1 inch apart on ungreased cookie sheets.

Bake at 375° in a preheated oven for 6 to 7 minutes or until edges are firm and bottoms are very light brown. Transfer cookies to wire racks to cool. Sprinkle with powdered sugar.

COOKIES

PUMPKIN COOKIES   Margaret Vowles

I found this pumpkin cookie recipe in the Bountiful 1ˢᵗ Ward cookbook, which was probably published in the 1950's. It was submitted by a widow by the name of Rose Burningham. Our family always enjoy these cookies although we substituted chocolate chips for raisins.

Years later while living in Centerville, a neighbor found out I had grown up in the 1ˢᵗ Ward. She said her grandmother was Rose Burningham. I told her I loved her grandmother's pumpkin cookie recipe. She asked if I had heard how the recipe came to be written down, and I said no. Rose did not have a written recipe, so her daughters had her make the cookies, and they carefully measured everything as she put the ingredients in the bowl.

2 c. brown sugar, firmly packed	2 1/2 tsp. baking powder
2 eggs	1/2 tsp. ginger
3/4 c. shortening	1/2 tsp. nutmeg
1 tsp. vanilla	1/2 tsp. cinnamon
1 1/2 c. cooked pumpkin	1/2 tsp. salt
2 1/2 c. flour	1/2 c. raisins

Cream shortening and sugar.   Beat well. Beat in eggs and vanilla.

Sift dry ingredients (except raisins).   Add to sugar mixture alternately with pumpkin. Add raisins.

Drop by spoonful on a greased cookie sheet.

Bake in a 350° oven for 18 minutes.

Makes 3 dozen.

COOKIES

SAND CAKES   Wendy Swanson
(Sandbakkels)

My great grandmother, Maren Karoline Helgensen Bjerke, who emigrated from Norway in 1909, taught her daughter-in-law (my grandmother) how to make these delicious treats. As a child, I did not know they were meant to be filled with something. We ate them so quickly; Grandma never had the chance to finish them.

1 c. unsalted butter   1 egg, well beaten
  (Do not use margarine!)   2 c. all-purpose flour
1/2 c. superfine (Baker's) sugar   1 tsp. vanilla or almond extract

Preheat oven to 375º. Use butter (or cooking spray) to lightly grease 2" *Sandbakkels tins.

Cream together the butter and sugar. Mix in the well-beaten egg followed by 2 cups of flour and 1 tsp. of flavoring. The soft batter should pull away from the sides of your mixing bowl; if not, add additional flour, 1 Tbsp. at a time, until it does.

With floured fingers, pinch off about 1 1/2 Tbsp. of dough. Roll into a ball, press into a tin, and use your thumbs to press the dough out to cover the bottom and sides of the tin in a thin layer. Repeat about 30 times.

Place tins on cookie sheet and bake on center rack of oven for 10 to 15 minutes (checking at 10 minutes. Their butter content causes these cookies to burn quickly).

Remove from oven and cool slightly. Turn the tins over on a baking rack or clean counter. If the tarts don't fall out of their own accord, tap lightly on the backs of the tins with a knife or spoon to loosen. Let tarts cool completely before filling.

If they last long enough, the tarts can be filled with custard, preserves, pie filling or fresh fruit.

*Sandbakkels tins

A secret grandma shared with me about these tins: Do not wash them in soap and water, but clean them out thoroughly with a lightly oiled cloth; otherwise, the next time you use them, your dough will stick.

COOKIES

SNICKERDOODLES   Wendy Swanson

1/2 c. butter, softened   1 c. granulated sugar
1/4 tsp. baking soda   1/4 tsp. cream of tartar
1 egg   1/2 tsp. vanilla
1 ½ c. all-purpose flour   2 Tbsp. sugar
1 tsp. ground cinnamon

In a medium mixing bowl beat butter with an electric mixer on medium to high speed for 30 seconds. Add the 1 cup of sugar, baking soda, and cream of tartar. Beat until combined, scraping sides of bowl occasionally. Beat in egg and vanilla. Beat in as much of the flour as you can with the mixer. Using a wooden spoon, stir in any remaining flour. Cover and chill in the refrigerator for 1 hour.

In a small mixing bowl combine the 2 tablespoons sugar and the cinnamon. Shape dough into 1-inch balls. Roll balls in the sugar-cinnamon mixture to coat. Place 2 inches apart on an ungreased cookie sheet.

Bake in a 375° F oven for 10 to 11 minutes or until edges are golden brown. Transfer cookies to a wire rack to cool.

COOKIES

SUPER SOFT SUGAR COOKIES   Joan Silver

1 c. butter (no substitutes)   2 tsp. vanilla
2 c. sugar   1/2 tsp. soda
2 eggs   4 tsp. baking powder
5 1/2 c. flour   1/2 tsp. salt
1 c. dairy sour cream (or plain yogurt)

Cream together butter and sugar. Add eggs and beat well. Add sour cream and vanilla.

Sift together dry ingredients and add to creamed mixture. Chill if desired.

Roll on floured surface 1/4 to 1/2 inch thick. Cut with cookie cutters.

Place on buttered cookie sheet about 2 inches apart. Bake at 350º for 6 to 12 minutes.

Cookies are large, soft, and thick. Frost, or sprinkle with sugar after baking.

COOKIES

SWEET & SALTY ZUCCHINI BREAD COOKIES   Wendy Swanson

3 1/3 c. flour
1 1/2 tsp. baking powder
1 1/2 tsp. salt
1 1/2 c. brown sugar
2 large eggs
1 c. grated zucchini
3/4 c. broken pretzels

1/3 c. cornstarch
1 1/4 tsp. baking soda
1 1/4 c. butter, softened
3/4 c. granulated sugar
1 Tbsp. vanilla
3/4 c. chopped cashews

In a medium bowl, whisk flour, cornstarch, baking powder, baking soda and salt.

In a large bowl, beat butter, brown sugar and granulated sugar until creamy. Beat in eggs one at a time. Beat in vanilla. Beat in flour mixture. Fold in zucchini, cashews and broken pretzels.

Drop dough by 1/3 cup scant scoopfuls onto cookie sheets, 1 inch apart.

Bake at 350° for 20 to 25 minutes or until bottoms are golden brown.

If you'd like, you can swap the zucchini for summer squash, and the cashews for peanuts.

SNACKS

SNACKS

88 CALORIE OATMEAL AND HONEY SNACK BALLS   Lucile Larson

1 c. oats (uncooked, regular or quick)
1/4 c. peanut butter
1/4 c. honey
1/4 c. dry roasted peanuts
1/4 c. mini M&M'S®
1/4 c. mini chocolate chips
Dash of salt
1/2 tsp. vanilla

Mix the PB and honey together. Add salt and vanilla. Stir in oats, M&M'S®
and chocolate chips.

Roll into 1-inch balls and refrigerate.

SNACKS

ADDICTION
Gail Ann Jacobsen

1 lg. box Rice Chex Cereal
4 c. large flake coconut
   (buy at Dixie Nutrition)
3 cubes butter
2 c. light Karo® syrup

1 lg. box Golden Grahams Cereal
3 c. sliced almonds

2 c. sugar

You will need a large area to complete.

Spread out wax paper (large amount) that has been sprayed with Pam® on your countertop or table – large area.

Combine cereals, coconut and almonds in a LARGE pan. Combine butter, sugar and Karo® syrup. Bring to a boil stirring often and boil for 3-5 minutes. Pour butter mixture over cereal and mix well. Spread out on the prepared wax paper.

Leave out overnight to dry. Break up and store in layers between wax paper in a covered container.

SNACKS

CARMEL POPCORN   Marlene Mason Wood

My Aunt Fonda Kennedy's recipe. She is one of my favorite aunts.

2 qts. popped corn
1 can Eagle Brand milk
1 lb. brown sugar (or 2 cups)
1 c. Karo® syrup
1 cube butter or margarine

Put milk, sugar and syrup in pan and mix together. Then put in butter. Bring to a boil and cook 3 minutes.

Pour the syrup slowly over the popped corn.

SNACKS

CEREAL MIX   Joan Silver

1 box each	Rice Chex™
	Corn Chex™
	Golden Grahams™
2 c. each	shredded coconut
	slivered almonds
3 c. butter	2 c. sugar
2 c. light Karo® syrup	1/2 tsp. vanilla

Mix dry ingredients in a large bowl. Bring butter, sugar and Karo® syrup to a boil for 5 minutes.

Add vanilla and pour over cereal and stir. Spread out to dry.

SNACKS

CINNAMON WALNUTS   Norma Dooley

This is a family favorite. We make them every Christmas.

1 c. granulated sugar	1 tsp. salt
6 Tbsp. canned milk	1 tsp. cinnamon
1/8 tsp. cream of tartar	1 tsp. vanilla
3 to 4 c. walnuts or almonds, or a mixture of both	

To make syrup, put all ingredients but walnuts in pan; heat and cook to soft ball stage (236° on candy thermometer).

Stir in walnuts. Spread on cookie sheet or out on counter top to cool and harden.

Break apart while still warm. Butter fingers if too sticky to handle.

Let cool completely and dry before putting in container.

Syrup scorches easily, so cook on medium to low heat and stir often.

SNACKS

GRANOLA   Joan Silver

Mix:

8 c. rolled oats	6 c. rolled wheat
2 c. untoasted wheat germ	2 – 3 c. coconut
2 tsp. salt	

Stir and heat until blended:

1 1/2 c. brown sugar	1 1/2 c. oil
1 c. honey	

Add 1 tsp. vanilla.

Combine all ingredients and roast at 250˚ for 1 hour; stir every 20 minutes.

SNACKS

POPCORN BALLS   Judy Call

1/2 c. light Karo® syrup	1/2 c. butter
1 c. sugar	1 tsp. salt
1 tsp. vanilla	1 tsp. food coloring - more or less
	Red or festive colors
1 tsp. cherry flavoring – more or less	4 qts. popped corn

Combine Karo® syrup, butter, sugar and salt. Stir over medium high heat until it reaches a good roiling boil. Turn off heat, cover with a lid and let set for 4 minutes. Add vanilla, coloring and flavoring; stir... slowly.

Pour over the popped corn. (A large plastic bowl is very hand.) Pour over small amount of corn, stirring and adding more corn, using only enough corn so syrup coats each kernel <u>well</u>.

You can shape into balls or lay out on a table to cool. *I have even wrapped them around a pop sucker.* After cooling, place in sandwich bags.

You can do many things with this scrumptious candied popcorn...
The important thing is to... EAT IT!!   YUM

SNACKS

SUGARED NUTS   Wendy Swanson

1 c. sugar
1/2 tsp. cinnamon
1/3 c. evaporated milk
1 1/2 c. nuts
1/2 tsp. vanilla

Boil sugar, cinnamon and milk to soft ball stage. Pour over nuts and vanilla. Stir until thoroughly coated. Spread out on wax paper to dry.

SNACKS

SUGARED POPCORN   Wendy Swanson

I got this recipe from my mom. I don't know who she got it from; she had written it in the margin above great-grandma's popcorn recipe; it is very good and easy to make.

2 qts. popped corn	1/2 c. water
2 c. sugar	1 tsp. vanilla

Combine sugar and water and cook, stirring constantly, until it becomes thready; about 5 minutes. Remove from heat and add vanilla.

Add the popcorn and stir to coat evenly.

Turn out onto parchment paper to cool. You can add a couple of drops of food coloring to make it look more festive.

CANDY

CANDY

DIVINITY
Wendy Swanson

My mother, Dixie Burke Warren, always makes the best divinity; thanks for sharing your recipe Mom!

3 c. sugar
1/2 c. cold water
1 tsp. vanilla

1/2 c. light corn syrup
2 egg whites

Place sugar, syrup and water in a pan over low heat. Stir only until sugar is dissolved; then cook until the mixture boils. Continue cooking over medium heat without stirring until it reaches the hard-ball stage. As it reaches the hard-ball stage, beat egg whites until stiff. Gradually pour hot syrup over egg whites, beating constantly at high speed of electric mixer. Add vanilla and continue beating until candy is thick enough to drop from a spoon (about 4 to 5 minutes). Walnut or pecan pieces can be added just before candy is ready to spoon. Drop by spoonful onto waxed paper. Once the candy is set, store in a tightly closed container. Makes about 36 pieces.

CANDY

GRACES CANDY   Gail Ann Jacobsen

This is a recipe that my Grandmother Beulah Browning made all of the time when she would visit. After my grandmother passed away, my mom would make it. It is a favorite of mine growing up. I treasure this recipe, not because I like to make it, but because it is in my mother's own hand writing.

3 c. sugar   1 c. milk
1 c. Karo® syrup (light)   2 Tbsp. butter
1 tsp. vanilla   Angel flake coconut

Mix sugar and milk together, bring to a boil. Add Karo® syrup. Cook to a firm ball stage. Remove from heat, add butter and vanilla. Beat until creamy. Add in Angel flake coconut.

Variation to the above:
Use 1 cup dark Karo® syrup instead of light syrup
Add 1 cup chopped walnuts
Add 1 tsp. maple flavoring **OR** 1 tsp. black walnut flavoring

CANDY

LICORICE CARAMEL   Joan Silver

2 c. sugar
1 can of Borden sweetened
   condensed milk

2 squares butter
1 1/2 c. white Karo® syrup
1 Tbsp. anise licorice flavor
   (paste – Wilton's)

In a large, heavy saucepan, mix together all ingredients except anise flavoring.

Stir constantly until firm ball. Then add anise licorice flavor.

MICROWAVE CARAMEL   Joan Silver

1/2 c. butter
1/2 c. Eagle brand condensed milk
1/2 c. white Karo® syrup

1/2 c. white sugar
1/2 c. brown sugar

Microwave on high for 7 minutes.

Fast and great!

CANDY

MILLION DOLLAR FUDGE   Joan Silver

I try to only make this on holidays, because it is so good.

4 1/2 c. white sugar	1 large can evaporated canned milk
1 cube butter	

In a large, heavy saucepan, mix together sugar, canned milk and butter. Bring to a boil and boil for 7 1/2 minutes.

Add: 1 large pkg. milk chocolate or semi-sweet chocolate chips

1 lb. Hershey bar	1 pt. marshmallow creme
1 tsp. vanilla	1 c. chopped nuts (if desired)

Pour into a 9 x 13" pan and cut when cool.

CANDY

NO FAIL FUDGE   Marlene Mason Wood

This recipe was given to me by my mother-in-law, Phyllis Wood, who was born June 2, 1917. Phyllis' mother did not teach her to cook, because her mother taught piano lessons to 85 students at one time, so they had a housekeeper. Phyllis learned to cook after she was married, by her mother-in-law.

1 cube butter or margarine	16 oz. chocolate chips
1 can of evaporated canned milk	1 pint marshmallow sauce
4 c. sugar	1 c. walnuts (small pieces)

In a large, heavy saucepan, mix together butter or margarine, canned milk and sugar. Bring to a boil and boil for 6 minutes, stirring constantly.

In a bowl; mix chocolate chips, marshmallow sauce and walnut pieces.

Add mixes together well. Pour in a pan lightly coated with cooking spray and let cool.

Enjoy!

CANDY

PINTO BEAN FUDGE   Gail Smith

Tasty treat using your food storage refried beans.

1 c. cooked soft pinto beans (drained and mashed). *I use the dry pack refried beans.*

1/4 c. milk   1 Tbsp. vanilla
6 oz. unsweetened chocolate   6 Tbsp. butter or margarine
2 lb. powdered sugar   Nuts (optional)

In large bowl stir beans and milk together, adding enough milk to resemble mashed potatoes, stir in vanilla. Melt chocolate and butter and stir into bean mixture. Gradually stir in powdered sugar.

Knead with hands to get it well blended. Spread into lightly buttered 9-inch baking dish or form into two 1 3/4" rolls. Chill 1-2 hours.

CANDY

PRALINE FUDGE   Wendy Swanson

This recipe comes from my mother-in-law, Gladys Buehre Swanson, whose mother taught her to make it. She passed before I had the chance to meet her, but I was able to get a copy of it from my sister-in-law, Victoria. This is my husband's favorite fudge, and I make it for him each year for Christmas. It's a little tricky to get it just right, but if it doesn't set, it makes a delicious topping for vanilla ice cream.

3 c. white sugar	1 pt. heavy whipping cream
1 c. white Karo® syrup	Dash of salt
1 Tbsp. vanilla	10 oz. pkg. pecans

In a large, heavy saucepan, boil on medium high heat; sugar, Karo syrup and whipping cream until it forms a firm, but not hard ball in cold water.

Cool, and then add pecans, salt and vanilla. Beat until shine is gone. Pour into a greased 8x8" pan. Cut into squares when set. For best storage, keep tightly covered.

Secret: *If your fudge is getting dry; add a few drops of water to the top and put in the microwave for about 10 seconds. This will work with any type of fudge.*

BEVERAGES

BEVERAGES

LAVENDER LEMONADE   Wendy Swanson

1 c. sugar
1 1/2 c. freshly squeezed lemon juice
2 c. boiling water
1 Tbsp. dried lavender or a small handful of freshly picked lavender
2 c. cold water
Ice cubes

Place the lavender in a large measuring bowl. Pour the sugar over the lavender and use your fingers to gently rub the lavender into the sugar.

Pour the boiling water over the sugar and stir until the sugar has melted. Cover and let infuse for at least 30 minutes. Now you have lavender infused simple syrup.

Strain the syrup and pour into a serving pitcher. Stir in the lemon juice and cold water. Taste and adjust for tartness; more lemon juice or more sugar.

Add ice cubes and serve.

BEVERAGES

SLUSH   Marlene Mason Wood

1 can (46 oz.) pineapple juice
1 can (6 oz.) frozen orange juice
3 bananas, mashed in a blender
2 Tbsp. lemon juice
4 c. sugar
8 c. water

Mix all ingredients together and freeze.

Pour 7UP® over when ready to serve according to how slushy you want it.

BEVERAGES

SPICY CRANBERRY PUNCH   Wendy Swanson

4 – 3" cinnamon sticks, broken
6 whole allspice berries
12 whole cloves
1 1/2 c. sugar
8 c. unsweetened cranberry juice (recipe on following page)
1 orange, sliced
1 qt. Sprite®

Tie spices together in a cheesecloth bag. In a large saucepan combine the cranberry juice, sliced orange and spice bag. Bring to boiling, reduce heat and simmer 20 minutes. Set aside to cool and discard spice bag and orange slices. Chill the cranberry juice.

Just before serving, pour juice into punch bowl, add the Sprite® and stir to blend. Garnish with additional orange slices if you wish. Makes 3 quarts.

If you want to use store-bought cranberry juice, omit the sugar.

BEVERAGES

FRESH CRANBERRY JUICE   Wendy Swanson

1 lb. fresh cranberries
3 c. water

In a large saucepan, pour the water over the fresh cranberries. Boil until the cranberries pop.

Drain off the juice and add enough water to make 4 cups.

If you want to use the cranberry juice to make the Spicy Cranberry Punch on the previous page, you'll need to make 2 recipes.

BEVERAGES

SPICY HOT CHOCOLATE　　　　　　　　　　　Wendy Swanson

This is a super quick and easy way to spice up your hot chocolate.

3 Tbsp. instant hot chocolate mix
1 Tbsp. Hershey's dark chocolate syrup
1/2 tsp. ground cinnamon
1 pinch chili powder
1/4 c. milk
3/4 c. boiling water

In a large mug, mix the hot chocolate mix, chocolate syrup, cinnamon, and chili powder. Pour in the milk. Add the boiling water and stir.

CANDY CANE HOT CHOCOLATE　　　　　　　　Wendy Swanson

Use the same recipe as above, but use one crushed peppermint candy cane instead of the cinnamon and chili powder.

216

JAMS & JELLIES

JAMS & JELLIES

FREEZER JAM (STRAWBERRY or RASPBERRY)   Wendy Swanson

This recipe and the one on the next page come from my great grandmother, Laura Martina Grieve Musgrave. My mother has her collection of recipes and many of the pages have become tattered and dog-eared from so much use.

2 c. mashed berries
4 c. sugar
1 pkg. pectin
1 c. water

Mix berries and sugar and let stand for 20 minutes, stirring occasionally.

Mix pectin and water together and bring to a boil. Boil 1 minute, stirring constantly. Remove from heat.

Add berries to pectin syrup and stir for two minutes.

Pour into small glass containers and cover tightly with lids.

Let stand 24 to 48 hours at room temperature. Place in freezer.

JAMS & JELLIES

FROZEN APRICOT JAM   Wendy Swanson

3 1/2 c. apricots
5 1/2 c. sugar
1/2 c. lemon juice
1 c. light corn syrup
1 pkg. pectin

Sort, wash and halve the apricots. Press fruit through a sieve into a bowl. Avoid stirring in air bubbles. Add lemon juice to the apricots to keep them from turning dark. Put sugar in a 4-quart cooking container and add apricots. Add corn syrup and pectin.

Cook until sugar is dissolved or 100 degrees (baby milk temperature).

Pour into small glass containers and cover tightly with lids. Freeze.

Washington Cotton Factory ~ Established 1865

MISCELLANEOUS

MISCELLANEOUS

ROSE JAR (or POTPOURRI)   Wendy Swanson

Gather the petals of roses and other sweet-smelling flowers in the early morning while the dew is still on. Spread the petals on a screen to dry off.

Place the petals in a one-gallon glass jar which has a tight-fitting lid, sprinkling 1/2" layer of petals with salt. Fill it halfway and set in a cool place for ten days, stirring every day.

Mix together 1 oz. each of ground cloves, cinnamon and allspice. Dump the petal mixture out of the jar and sprinkle the bottom of the jar with the spice mixture. Keep adding a layer of petals and sprinkle with spice until the spices and petals have been used up. Set jar in a cool place for three weeks.

The final step is to have assembled 1/4 oz. each of mace, nutmeg, cloves and allspice; 1/2 oz. cinnamon, 1 oz. orris root, 4 oz. lavender flowers, 1 oz. rose geranium leaves, 1 oz. lemon verbena, and any other spice or died and powdered sweet-scented leaves.

Dump out the jar again and add alternate layers of spice and petals. Jar should be filled only halfway. If you'd like, add 1 oz. of any good perfume, taking care not to make the mixture overly wet.

Open the jar for about a half hour and it will scent the entire room.

A rose jar made using this method will still be fragrant 50 years from now!

MISCELLANEOUS

SOAP   Wendy Swanson

This is my great grandmother, Laura Martina Grieve Musgrave's recipe. When my mother was a child, her parents would sometimes take her and her brothers and sister to their grandmother's house for the weekend. She lived in an old farmhouse in the country with no running water or indoor plumbing. The children would take turns bathing in a large metal tub in the kitchen on Saturday night. This was the soap she used.

10 c. grease
1 can lye
1/2 c. Borax
1/2 c. powdered amonia

Wash grease to remove dirt and salt. Pour lye in an enamel-ware pan (Do not use aluminum metal pans) and add 5 cups of water. Let cool to room temperature and add the softened grease (not melted) and stir with a stick or wooden paddle. Add Borax and ammonia and continue to stir now and then until almost hard. Dump into a paper carton. Let stand for a day or so and then grind and put away in a container for future use. If the odor of ammonia is objectionable, 1/2 c. of White King Water Softener may be substituted. Some folks like to add a little Vel or Tide for a sudsier soap.

MISCELLANEOUS

The following recipes are only for the adventurous, and we are not recommending them! Silkworm pupae also called "Beondegi" is a popular snack food found in grocery stores and at street vendors in South Korea. It first became popular during the Korean War. The silkworms were readily available and gave the people a steady supply of nutritional protein.

CANDIED SILKWORM PUPAE

1 1/2 c. silkworm pupae   1/2 c. brown sugar

Line a baking sheet with parchment paper. Place pupae in oven 10 minutes at 400°. Mix pupae and brown sugar together in a large saucepan and set on a stove-top over medium to medium-high heat. As the brown sugar melts, use a wooden spoon to move the mixture around in the saucepan, making sure that all of the pupae get coated and none of the sugar stays in one place long enough to burn. Cook for about 5 minutes at the most, until all of the sugar has melted and all of the pupae are coated (or immediately if you smell anything burning).

Then, remove from heat and quickly spread the pupae out on the lined baking sheet to prevent them from drying in a clump. Allow pupae to cool for about a minute before eating or adding to a recipe.

ROASTED SILKWORM PUPAE

1 can silkworm pupae	1 Tbsp. soy sauce
1 Tbsp. Sriracha hot sauce	1 tsp. sesame oil
2 garlic cloves, finely minced	Salt to taste

Drain the canned silkworm pupae then soak for 1 hour in cold water to eliminate the canned metallic taste. Drain and repeat the process two more times. After the last soak pat dry with paper towel.

Combine the soy sauce, Sriracha hot sauce, sesame oil and garlic cloves.

Marinate the pupae in the sauce for 30 minutes. Line a baking sheet with parchment paper and preheat your oven to 400°.

Drain the pupae of excess marinade and evenly scatter on the baking sheet. Place in the oven and roast 45-60 minutes or until light and crisp. Give the baking sheet a shake every 10 minutes or so to ensure even roasting. When done, sprinkle to taste with salt.

Note: Canned silkworm pupae is available at Amazon.com and Ebay.

Relief Society Hall, Washington, Utah

Historic Marker

ZCMI Co-op Building
1872-1875

Official outlet of ZCMI (Zion's Co-operative Mercantile Institution), "America's First Department Store". This building housed the Zions Co-op Rio Virgin Manufacturing Company from 1872-1875. It was part of the ZCMI co-operative system which served more than 150 communities in the Intermountain area with retail commodities and services beginning in 1868.

EMERGENCY SUBSTITUTIONS

Emergency Substitutions

It's always best to use the ingredients specified in a recipe, but when you're in a bind, these hints may save you a trip to the grocery store.

For	*Use*
1 Tbsp. cornstarch	2 Tbsp. all-purpose flour
1 tsp. baking powder	1/4 tsp. baking soda + 1/2 tsp. cream of tartar
1 c. buttermilk	1 Tbsp. vinegar + 1 c. milk (let stand for 5 min.)
1 c. corn syrup	1 c. granulated sugar + 1/4 c. water
1 c. brown sugar	3/4 c. white sugar + 1/2 c. molasses
1 c. honey	1 1/4 c. granulated sugar + 1/4 c. water
1 oz. unsweetened chocolate	3 Tbsp. cocoa + 1 Tbsp. butter or margarine
1 tsp. lemon peel	1 tsp. lemon extract
1 c. cream	1/2 c. butter + 3/4 c. milk
1 c. sour cream	1 c. yogurt
1 c. oil (for baked goods)	1 c. applesauce
1 c. shortening (for baked goods)	1 1/8 c. butter or margarine, minus- 1/2 tsp. salt in recipe
1 c. Marshmallow Creme	16 large marshmallows + 2 Tbsp. corn syrup (melted in a double boiler)
1 Tbsp. fresh herbs	1 tsp. dried

INDEX

Appetizers & Condiments cont'd:

Soups & Stews:

Salads & Side Dishes:

Salads & Side Dishes cont'd:

Breads & Rolls:

Main Dishes:

Main Dishes cont'd:

Desserts:

Desserts cont'd:

Cookies:

Cookies cont'd:

Snacks:

Candy:

Beverages:

Jams & Jellies:

Miscellaneous

Emergency Substitutions

Made in the USA
Lexington, KY
06 December 2019